Haseang

GW00645485

Robin Davis • Günter Gerngross • Christian Holzmann • Herbert Puchta

Acknowledgements

The authors would like to express their thanks to a large number of people who have all contributed in some way to the final shape of this book:

Dir. Edith Rainer for assisting us enormously with her excellent word-processing skills and for her patience and support.
Erich Ballinger, whose creative ideas and drawings we feel have given the book a very stimulating appearance.
Mario Bottazzi, whose musical talents combined with pedagogical expertise have put a lot of fun into grammar practice.
Mag. Günter Schardinger for his computer-programming skills, which enabled us to monitor and control vocabulary input and progression.
Mag. Ruth Havas for her support to the team and her untiring editorial commitment to the project.
Birgit Zepf for her professional desktop-publishing expertise.
Chris Inman for his meticulous native-speaker check, James Richardson and the staff of AVP Studios, London, for the sound recordings and Andrew Ward for the photographs.
Bell College, Saffron Walden, for allowing us to hold authors' meetings in the college and use their extensive materials resources.
The many colleagues whose comments have been invaluable in the writing of this book.
Last but not least thanks to the 23 teachers who have been involved in the official trials of our material and whose feedback has been extremely useful.
And, as always, our families for their everlasting support and their patience.

Günter Gerngroß
Herbert Puchta
Robin Davis
Christian Holzmann

CONTENTS

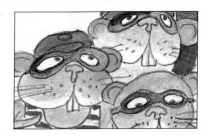

Indicates texts or exercises on the cassette.

★ Indicates exercises that are more demanding.

Welcome to English

1 A song

Listen to the song.

English is a word game

English is a word game.
English is a word game.
Come on, play English with me.

English is a word game.
English is a word game.
Come on, play English with me.

English is a word game.
English is a word game.
It's a game for you and me.

Do you speak English?
No.
I say yes.
What?
Listen:

Video, computer, Game Boy, Walkman,
Donald Duck, Hollywood, hamburger,
Disneyland, highway, mountain bike,
USA, rock 'n' roll, swimming pool,
hot dog, orange juice, Sky Channel,
four-wheel drive, basketball,
disco dancing.

English is a word game.
English is a word game.
Come on, play English with me.

English is a word game.
English is a word game.
It's a game for you and me.

Hey everybody, hey everybody,
sing this song, sing this song,
sing this song for you and me.

English is a word game.
English is a word game.
Come on, play English with me.

Skateboard, volleyball,
the White House,
Mickey Mouse, space shuttle,
racing car, airport, superstar.

English is a word game.
English is a word game.
Come on, play English with me.

English is a word game.
English is a word game.
Come on, play English with me.

2

Look at the pictures. Fill in the words you know.

3 Picture dictionary

4 Look and write the numbers.

one	orange
	cameras
	T-shirts
	stars
	cats
	rings
	bananas
	mountain bikes
	clowns
	pizzas
	hamburgers
	socks

5 Listen and fill in the telephone numbers.

Janet		Kate	
Steven		Patrick	

6 Ask four children in class and take notes.

What's your telephone number, Suzie?
6-0-4-7-9-5

Name				
Phone number				

7 *Follow the lines.*

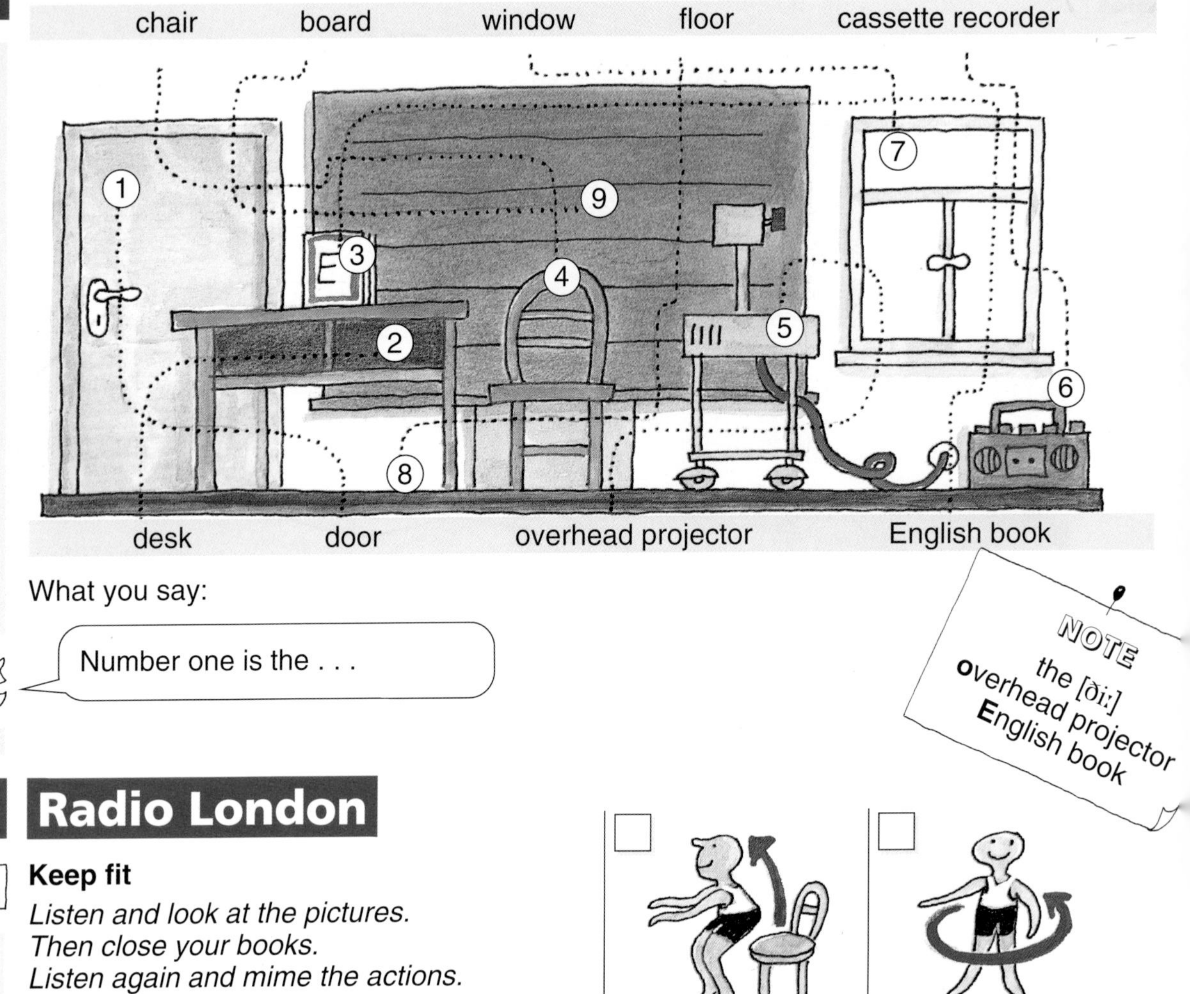

What you say:

8 Radio London

Keep fit

Listen and look at the pictures.
Then close your books.
Listen again and mime the actions.

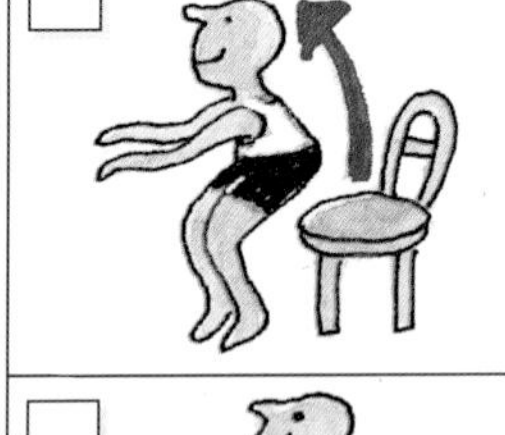

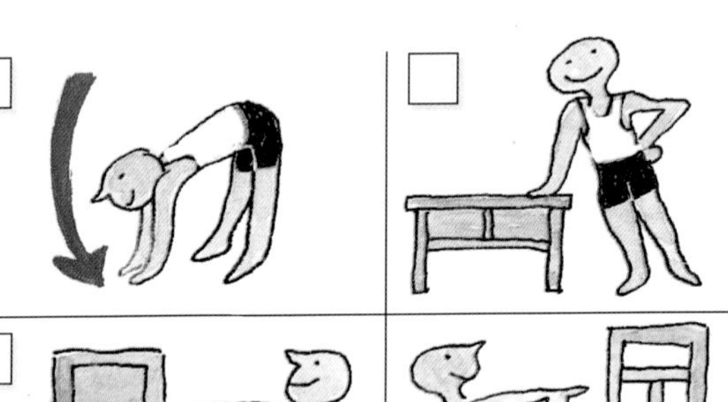

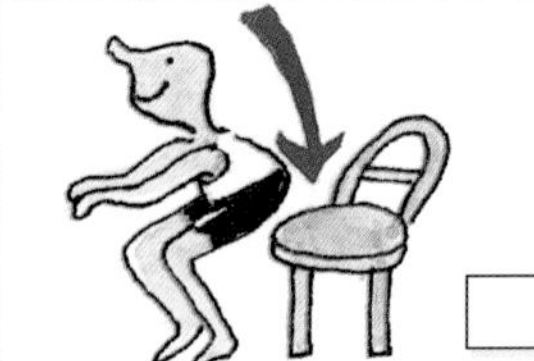

9 *Take a pencil.*
Listen and look at the pictures again.
Fill in the numbers.

10 A song

Fill in the telephone numbers.

What's your telephone number?

What's your telephone number?
Tell me, tell me, Kate.
What's your telephone number?
Is it __ - __ - __ - __ - __ ?

Okay, stand up and turn around,
I'll write it on your back.
__ - __ - __ - __ - __ - __ ,
that's it, that's it, Jack.

What's your telephone number?
Tell me, tell me, Sue.
What's your telephone number?
Is it __ - __ - __ - __ - __ ?

Okay, stand up and turn around,
I'll write it on your back.
__ - __ - __ - __ - __ - __ ,
that's it, that's it, Jack.

NOTE
what is = what's
it is = it's
that is = that's
857

11

Colour the picture.

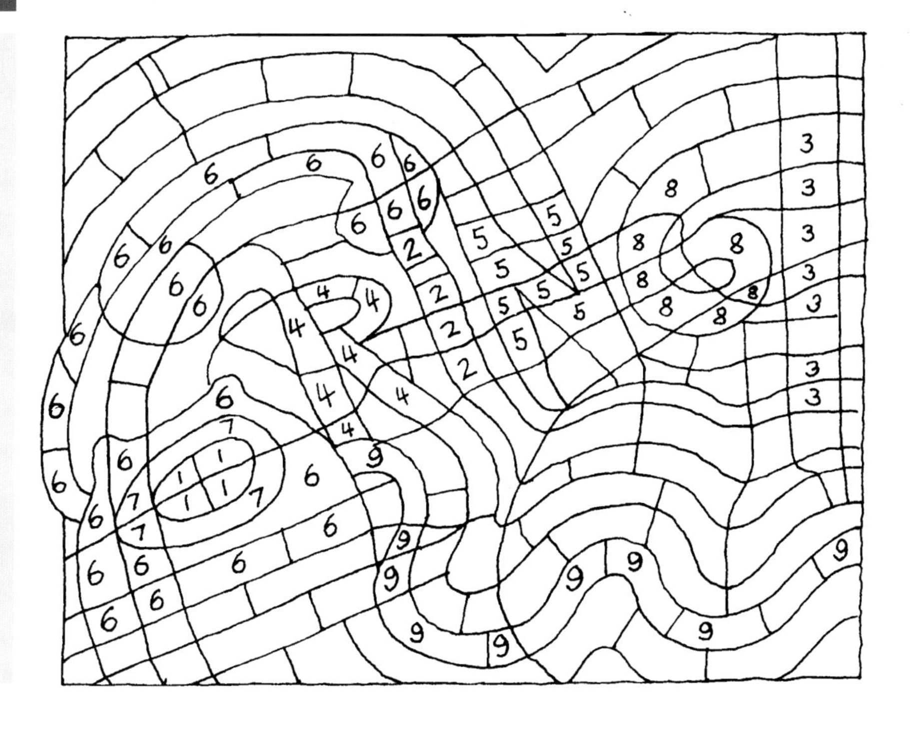

1 pink
2 green
3 blue
4 yellow
5 orange
6 red
7 grey
8 brown
9 black

12 *Colour the things on T-shirt number 1. Then ask your partner the questions below. Colour T-shirt number 2.*

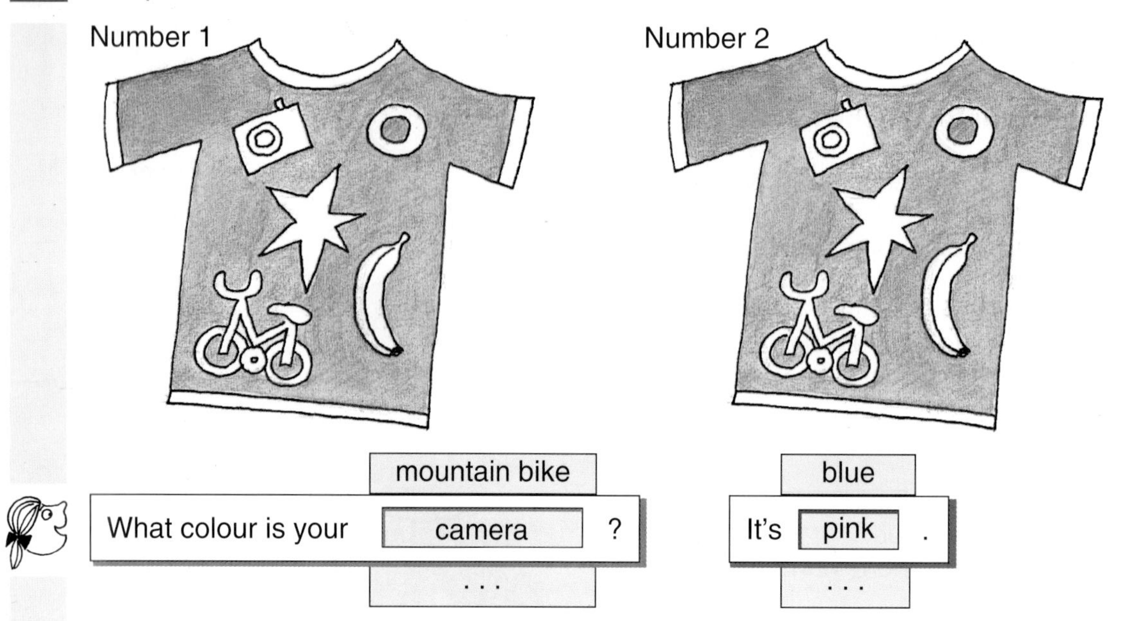

13 **Goblins in the classroom**

It's midnight. *Listen and colour.*

Grammar

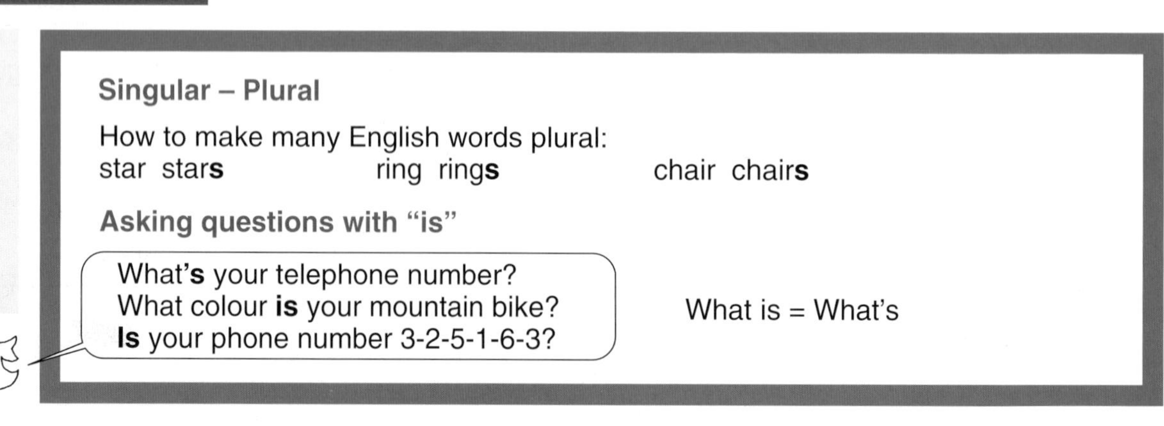

Singular – Plural

How to make many English words plural:

star star**s** ring ring**s** chair chair**s**

Asking questions with "is"

What'**s** your telephone number?
What colour **is** your mountain bike?
Is your phone number 3-2-5-1-6-3?

What is = What's

Sweets and snacks

1 Picture dictionary

2

Listen and fill in the numbers.

ice creams		hamburgers	
toffees		apples	
fruit gums		hot dogs	
oranges		sweets	

3 Grammar rhythm

Listen and fill in: ***a*** *or* ***an***

apple – an apple
banana – _____ banana
orange – _____ orange
sandwich – _____ sandwich
yummy, yummy, yummy
yummy, yummy, yummy

sweet – _____ sweet
lolly – _____ lolly
toffee – _____ toffee
ice cream – _____ ice cream
toothache, toothache
Ouch!

Listen and fill in the missing words.
Then do the rhythms in class.

Do you want a ____________?
Yes, please. Yes, please.
Do you want a ____________?
Yes, please. Yes, please.
Do you want a ____________?
Yes, please. Yes, please.

Do you want an ____________,
a ____________ or an ____________?
No, thanks. No, thanks.
What do you want? What do you want?
A toothbrush. A toothbrush.

4

Read and act out dialogues.

Flavours	
ice cream	chewing gum
vanilla	spearmint
strawberry	juicy fruit
chocolate	peppermint

5

Read and act out dialogues.

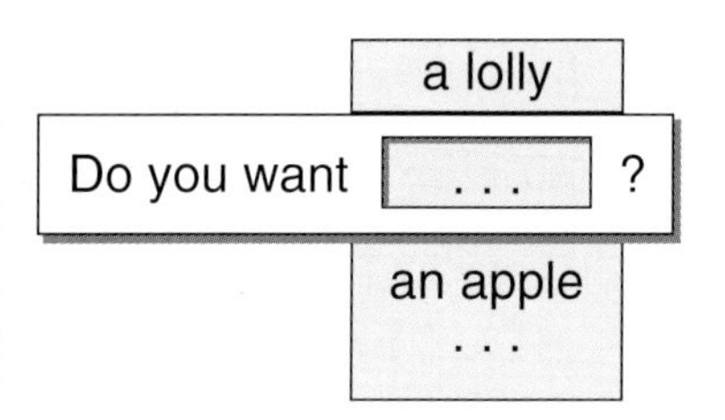

6

Listen and fill in the words.
Then act out the dialogue.

Kim: ____________, Mark?
Mark: Yes, please.
Kim: Here you are.
Mark: Thank you.
Kim: Do you want one, Sylvia?

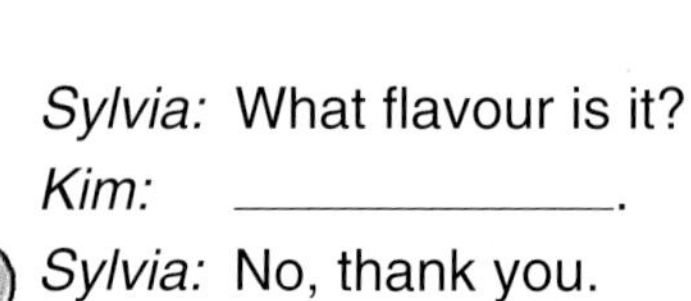

Sylvia: What flavour is it?
Kim: ____________.
Sylvia: No, thank you. I hate peppermint.

7 Radio London

Learn through mime

Listen and look at the pictures. Then close your books.
Listen again and mime the actions.

8

Take a pencil.
Listen and look at the pictures again.
Fill in the numbers.

9

Tell your partner what you like or hate.

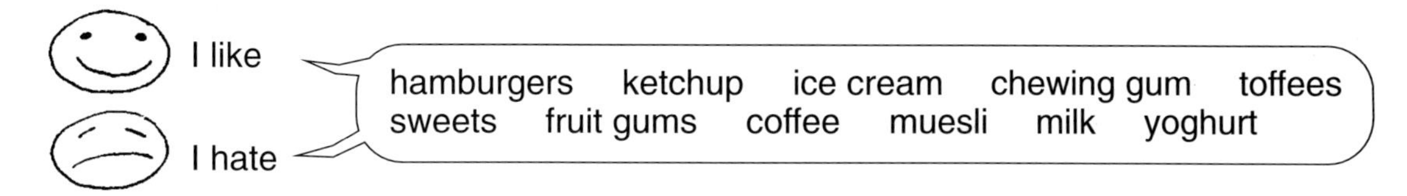

I like
I hate
hamburgers ketchup ice cream chewing gum toffees
sweets fruit gums coffee muesli milk yoghurt

10

Ask your partner and fill in the answers (+ or –).

Your partner:

Yes, I do.
No, I don't.

You:

Do you like . . .?

11 A sketch

Listen. Then act out the sketch.

Grammar

a – an

a	banana sandwich hamburger
an	apple orange ice cream

Watch out! Whether you use **a** or **an** depends on the sound the following word begins with.

Do you like . . .?

How to ask if someone likes something:

Do you like bananas?

Yes, I do.

No, I don't.

Do you want . . .?

How to offer something:

Yes, please.

Do you want a toffee?

No, thank you.

It's party time

1 Picture dictionary

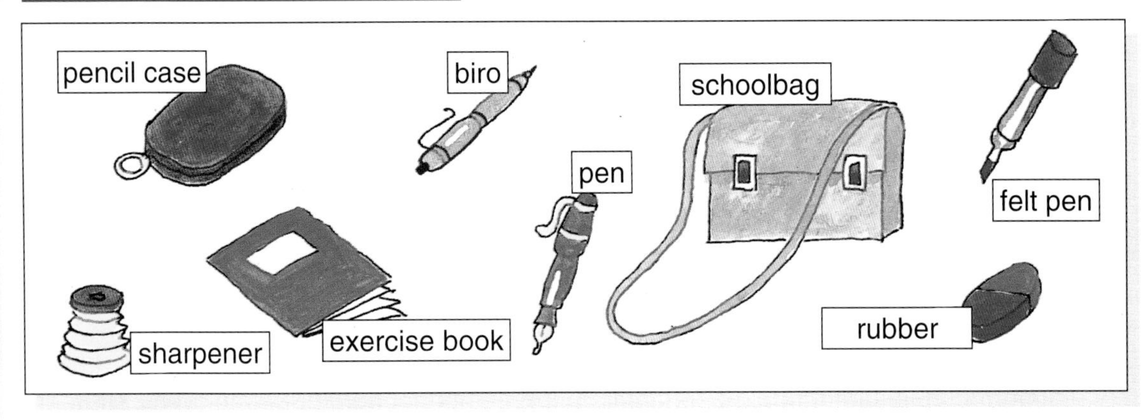

2

Listen to the cassette. Draw lines.

3 *Listen to the story. Fill in the names from the box.*

Tony Rick Pam Cathy Jenny Tina

Sarah's party

Sarah is on her way home from school.

She meets her friend __________.
"Let's have a party," Sarah says.
"A party?" __________ asks.
"Yes, it's the beginning of the school year."
"Good idea," __________ says.

Sarah and __________ meet __________.
"Let's have a party," Sarah and __________ say.
"A party?" __________ asks.
"Yes, it's the beginning of the school year."
"Good idea," __________ says.

Sarah, __________ and __________ meet __________.
"Let's have a party," Sarah, __________ and __________ say.
"A party?" __________ asks.
"Yes, it's the beginning of the school year."
"Good idea," __________ says.

Sarah, __________, __________ and __________ meet __________.
They meet Jim, they meet __________,
they meet Monica, and they meet __________.
And they all come to the party.
At five o'clock Sarah's garden is full of her friends.
The party is great fun!

NOTE
Sarah meet**s** a friend.
Sarah say**s** hallo.

4 Grammar rhythm

Forms of "to be". *Listen and fill in.*

Singular	1. Person		I am
	2. Person		
	3. Person		
Plural	1. Person		
	2. Person		
	3. Person		

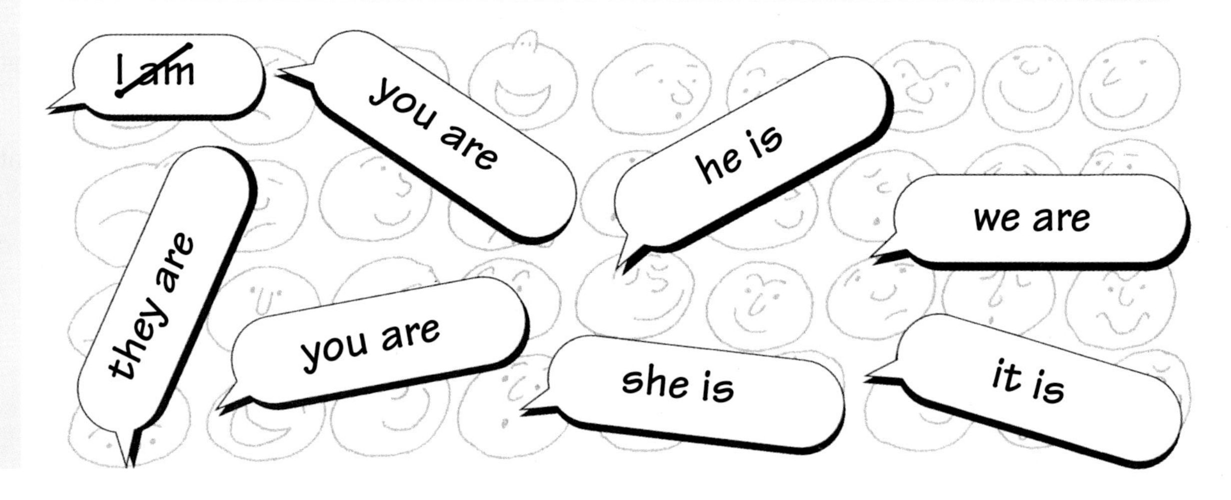

5 Picture dictionary

6 Grammar rhythm

"To be" with an adjective. *Listen and fill in.*

I am happy.

You ______.

He ______.

She ______.

Brrr. It ______.

We ______.

You ______.

They ______.

7 A song

Let's have a party

Let's have a party.
Let's have a party.
Yeah, a party is great fun.
Come to my party.
Come to my party.
Yeah, a party is great fun.

Hi, I'm Jenny. This is Tom.
Hallo, Tom. Let's sing a song.

Let's have a party.
Let's have a party.
Yeah, a party is great fun.
Come to my party.
Come to my party.
Yeah, a party is great fun.

Hallo, I'm Mary. This is John.
Hallo, John. Let's sing a song.

Let's have a party.
Let's have a party.
Yeah, a party is great fun.
Come to my party.
Come to my party.
Yeah, a party is great fun.

Thank you for the cake.
It's lovely.
I'm hungry,
he's hungry,
she's hungry,
we're hungry.
Let's cut the cake.
Mmh, it's great. Yummy.

Oh, it's a great party.
It's a great party.
Yeah, my party is great fun.
What a great party.
What a great party.
Yeah, my party is great fun.

8 Sarah's garden is full of her friends.
Fill in the speech bubbles.

Hallo, Cathy. Are you alright? Yes. Great.

Hallo, Cathy. This is my friend Danny. Hallo, Danny.

How are you, Mike? Fine, thank you, Mrs Clark.

9 Sarah's mother says hallo to Sarah's friends.
Listen to the dialogues and act them out.

Mum. This is Bill.
Hallo, Bill.
Hallo, Mrs Clark.

Are you alright, Monica?
I'm fine, thanks.
Great party?
Yes, it's great.

Hi! I'm Tony.
Oh hallo, Tony. How are you?
Very well, thank you, Mrs Clark.

Grammar

Forms of "to be"

I am happy.
You are late.
He is hungry.
She is great.
It is cold.
We are sleepy.
You are late.
They are tall.

Questions

Are you OK?
Is he hungry?
Is she happy?
Is it cold?
Are we late?
Are you hungry?
Are they tall?

Possessive

How to say that something belongs to someone:

Sarah**'s** pen
Tom**'s** biro
Cathy**'s** pencil case
Rick**'s** exercise book

UNIT 4

CLOTHES

1 Picture dictionary

2

Look at the picture dictionary for one minute. Then close your books. Work with a partner. A says a word from the picture dictionary. B says the words on either side of A's word.

3

13	14	15	16	17	18	19	20
thirteen	fourteen	fifteen	sixteen	seventeen	eighteen	nineteen	twenty

30	40	50	60	70	80	90	100
thirty	forty	fifty	sixty	seventy	eighty	ninety	a hundred

4 Take a pencil. Listen, tick ✔ and draw lines.

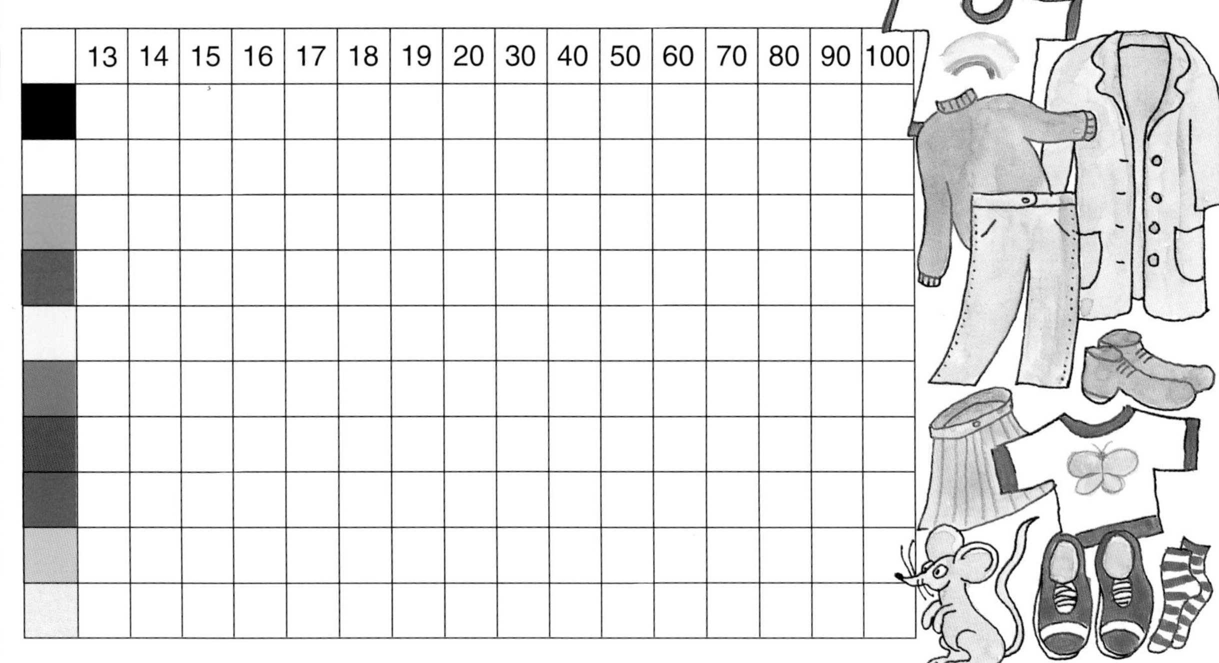

	13	14	15	16	17	18	19	20	30	40	50	60	70	80	90	100

5 Look, read and write.

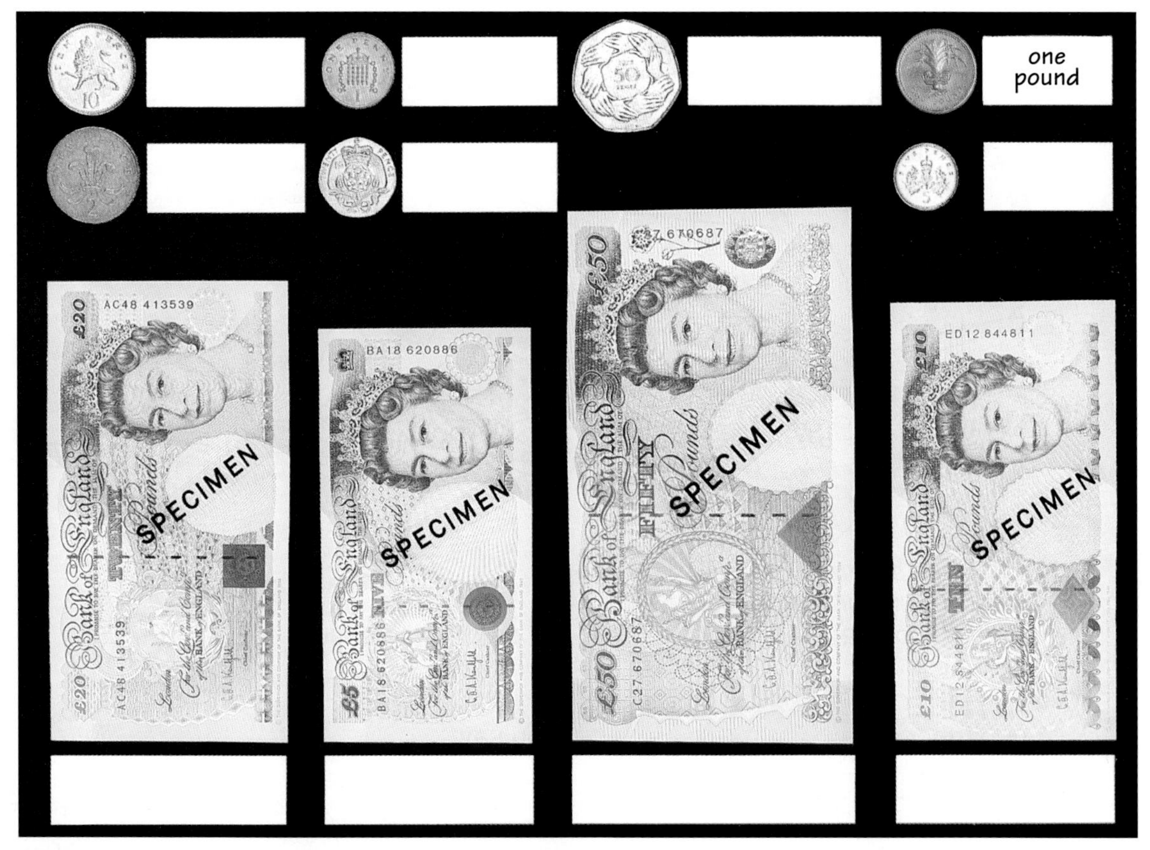

Coins: 1 penny, 2 pence, 5 pence,10 pence, 20 pence, 50 pence, 1 pound
Bank notes: 5 pounds, 10 pounds, 20 pounds, 50 pounds

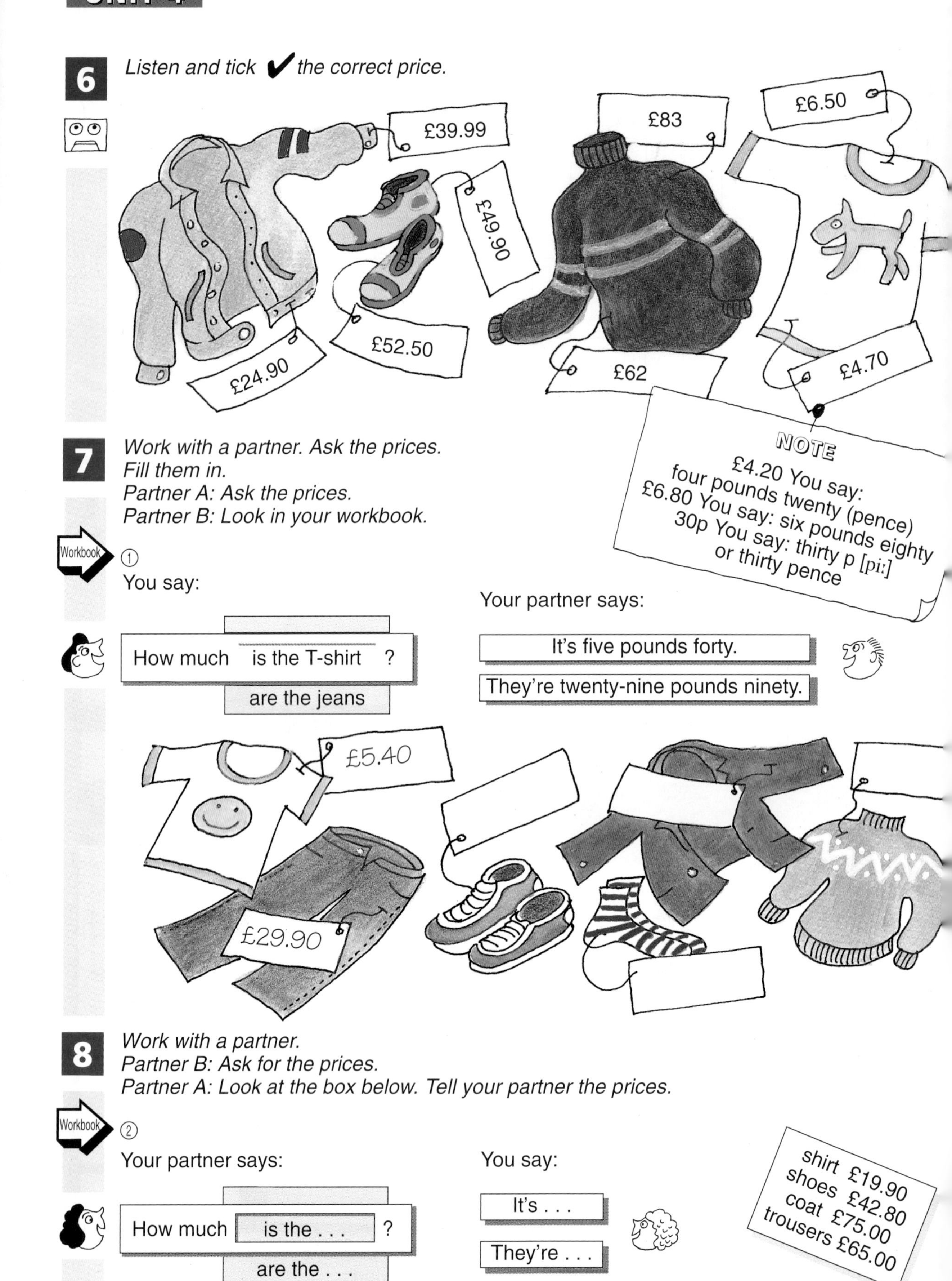
6
Listen and tick ✔ the correct price.
£39.99
£83
£6.50
£49.90
£24.90
£52.50
£62
£4.70
7
Work with a partner. Ask the prices.
Fill them in.
Partner A: Ask the prices.
Partner B: Look in your workbook.
NOTE
£4.20 You say:
four pounds twenty (pence)
£6.80 You say: six pounds eighty
30p You say: thirty p [pi:]
or thirty pence
Workbook
①
You say:
Your partner says:
How much
is the T-shirt
are the jeans
?
It's five pounds forty.
They're twenty-nine pounds ninety.
£5.40
£29.90
8
Work with a partner.
Partner B: Ask for the prices.
Partner A: Look at the box below. Tell your partner the prices.
Workbook
②
Your partner says:
You say:
How much
is the . . .
are the . . .
?
It's . . .
They're . . .
shirt £19.90
shoes £42.80
coat £75.00
trousers £65.00

9 A song

How much . . . ?

How much is the T-shirt?
Tell me, how much is it?
It's three pounds ninety-nine.

Aha,
how much are the jeans?
Tell me, how much are they?
They're thirteen pounds ninety-nine.

And,
how much is the jacket?
Tell me, how much is it?
It's thirty pounds ninety-nine.

Oh,
how much are the trainers?
Tell me, how much are they?
They're thirty-three pounds ninety-nine.

Oh no! How much is the sweater?
Tell me, how much is it?
It's ninety-nine pounds ninety-nine.

Sorry, so sorry.
I've got ninety-nine pence,
but I haven't got a pound.

10

Listen and write.

_____ + _____ = ☐

_____ – _____ = ☐

_____ – _____ = ☐

_____ + _____ = ☐

_____ – _____ = ☐

11

At the market

Act out dialogues.

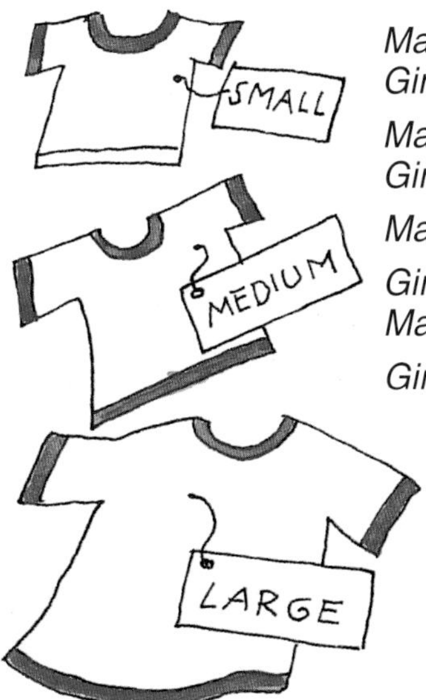

Man: Can I help you?
Girl: A red T-shirt, please.

Man: Small or medium?
Girl: Small.

Man: Here you are.

Girl: How much is it?
Man: Six pounds ninety.

Girl: OK, I'll take it.

12 Radio London

Learn through mime

Listen and look at the pictures. Then close your books.
Listen again and mime the actions.

13

Take a pencil.
Listen and look at the pictures again.
Fill in the numbers.

Grammar

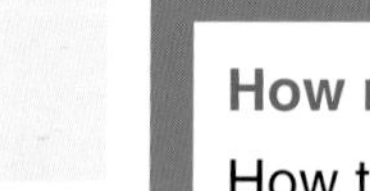

How much is . . .? – How much are . . .?

How to ask how much something costs:

How much **is** the pen?

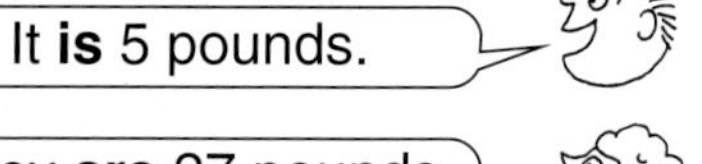

How much **are** the trainers?

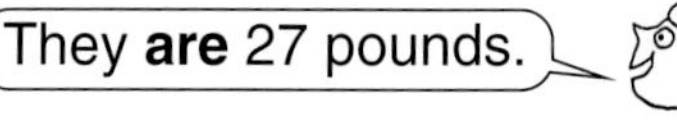

In an English classroom

1 Listen to the cassette. Fill in the numbers in the pictures.

Then write the correct numbers against the sentences.

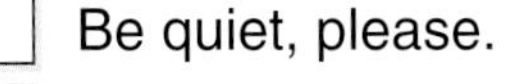

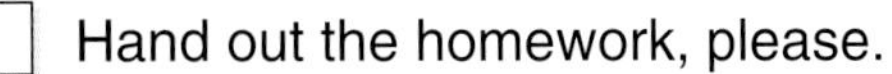

- [ ] Take out your textbooks.
- [ ] Copy the sentences.
- [ ] Clean the board, please.
- [ ] Listen to the cassette.
- [ ] Be quiet, please.
- [ ] Hand out the homework, please.
- [ ] Shut your books.
- [ ] Open the window, please.

Classroom English

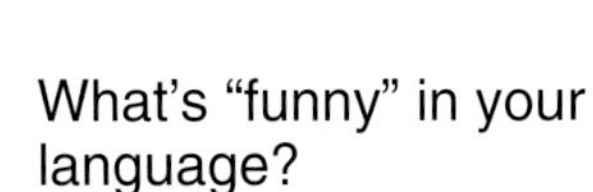

Sorry, I don't understand.
Pardon?

What's "..." in English

What's "funny" in your language?

What's the homework please?

2 Read Karen's letter.

Dear Barbara,
Here is a photo of our school. I am in 1b. We all wear uniforms to school: a dark blue skirt, a white blouse, a dark blue pullover, a red school tie, a dark blue blazer and black shoes.
I do not like school uniforms very much. I think they look boring.
What do you think?
Yours, Karen

3 Work with a partner. Say what you think.

nice

I think school uniforms look okay.

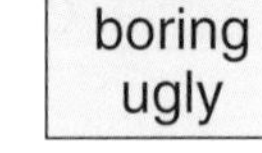

I think so too.

I don't think so.

sweaters
jeans
skirts

So do I.

I like wearing trainers to school.

shoes
T-shirts
blazers
. . . and . . .

I don't. I like wearing . . .

4 Radio London

Keep fit

Listen and look at the pictures.
Then close your books. Listen again. Mime the actions.

5

Take a pencil.
Listen and look at the pictures again.
Fill in the numbers.

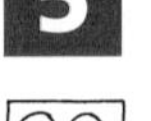

6 A song

Sing and mime the actions.

The funny teacher

He's a very funny teacher.
Yes, he is.
He's a very funny teacher.
Yes, he is.
Is he new at our school?
Yes, he is.
Is he really so cool?
Yes, he is.

His eyes are blue,
his name is Sunny,
and what he says is always funny:
Don't iron your books.
Don't bite the chair.
Don't sit on the board.
Don't write on your hair.

He's a very funny teacher.
Yes, he is.
He's a very funny teacher.
Yes, he is.
Is he new at our school?
Yes, he is.
Is he really so cool?
Yes, he is.

His eyes are blue,
his name is Sunny,
and what he says is always funny.
He's a very funny teacher.
Yes, he is.
He's a very funny teacher.
Yes, he is.
He's a very funny teacher.
Yes, he is.

Study and change

Text 1

I like our school. I am in 1 b.
We do not wear
school uniforms.
I like wearing my
blue jeans, my red T-shirt
and my red and green
sweater to school.

Text 2

Our school is OK. I am in 1 a.
I think school uniforms look nice,
but in our school we do not wear
school uniforms. I like wearing jeans
and trainers to school. I do not like
wearing skirts.

Grammar

Imperatives

How to tell someone to do or not to do something:

Listen, please.
Open your book.
Be quiet, please.

Don't open the book.
Don't open the window, please.
Don't turn around.

Circus, circus

1 *Fill in the words from the box.*

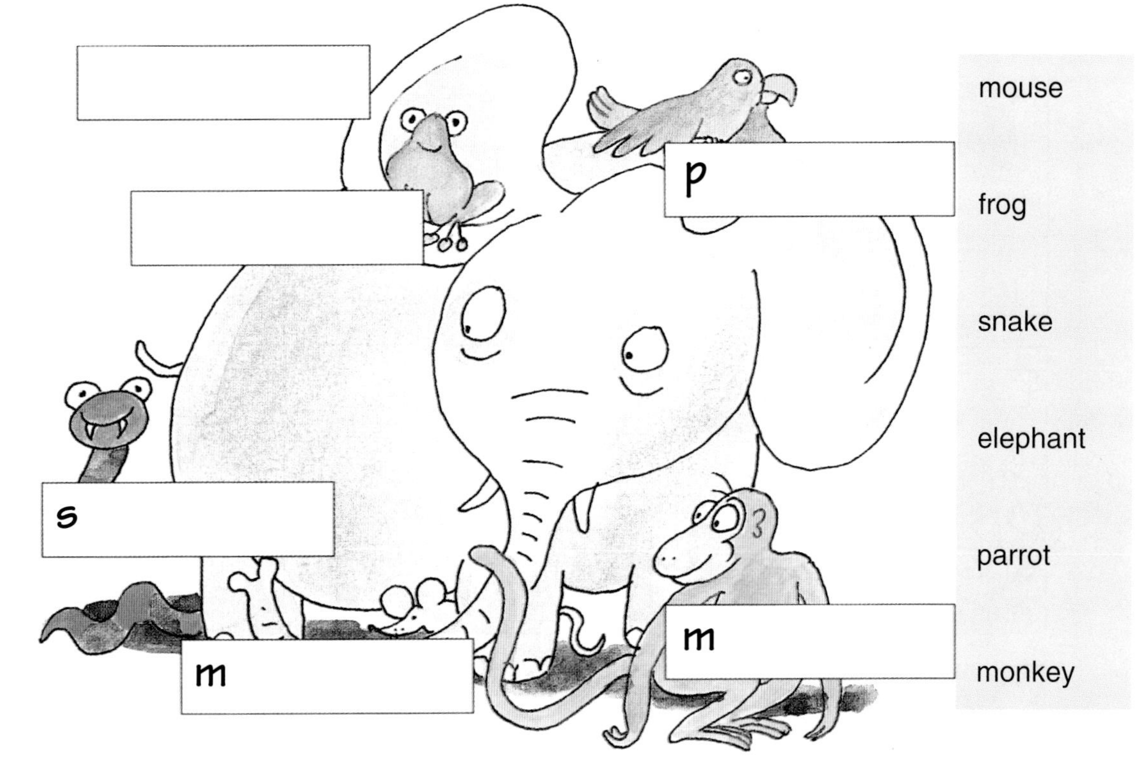

2 *Look at the picture in **1** for a minute. Then cover it up. Answer your teacher's questions.*

Your teacher:

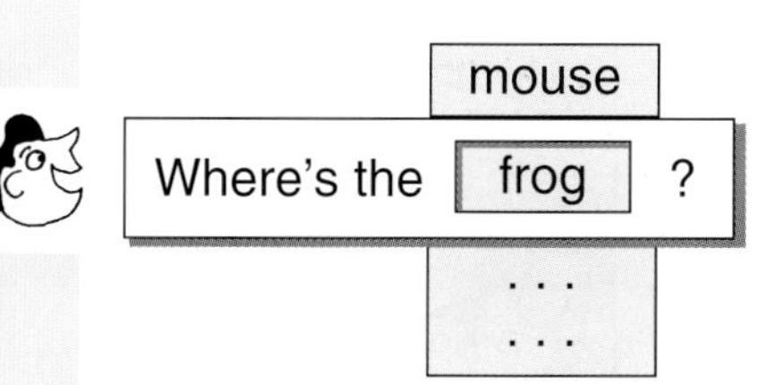

You:

in front of
It's behind the elephant.
under

It's in the elephant's ear .
on back

3 Listen to the story. Then put the pictures in the right order. Fill in the numbers 1 to 15.

4 Listen to the circus story again. Fill in the blanks.

Circus director: Monkey, monkey.
Monkey: What is it?
Circus director: Take the ____________ to the snake.
Monkey: Where is the ____________ ?
Circus director: ____________ the caravan.
Monkey: Alright. Alright.
Yummy. I ____________ hamburgers.

Circus director: Monkey, monkey.
Monkey: What is it?
Circus director: Take the ____________ to the parrot.
Monkey: Where is the ____________ ?
Circus director: ____________ the caravan.
Monkey: Alright. Alright.
Yummy. I love apples.

Circus director: Monkey, monkey.
Monkey: What is it?
Circus director: Take the ____________ to the mouse.
Monkey: Where is the mouse?
Circus director: ____________ the caravan.
Monkey: Alright. Alright.
Yummy. Yummy. Chocolate.
I love chocolate.

Circus director: Monkey, monkey.
Monkey: What is it?
Circus director: Take the ____________ to the frog.
Monkey: Where is the ____________ ?
Circus director: ____________ the caravan.
Monkey: Alright. Alright.
Yummy. I love toffees.
Toffees are wonderful.

Animals: Where is the food? We are ____________ .
Circus director: You are hungry? Where is the monkey?
Animals: Catch the thief. Catch the thief.
Monkey: Help! Help!

5 Listen to the story again.
Then act it out.

6 *"Hide" the animals and write the letters in the picture. Do not look at your partner's book.*

7 *Ask your partner.*

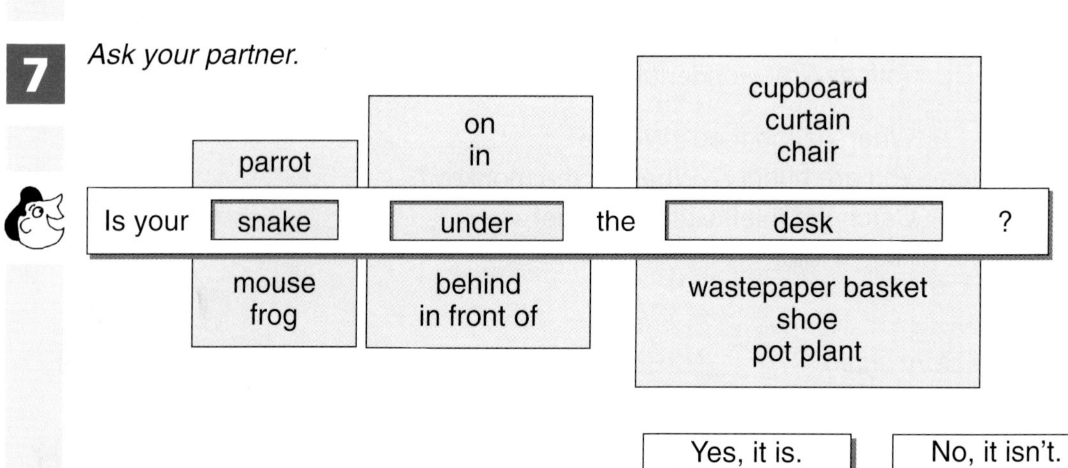

parrot
on
in
cupboard
curtain
chair
Is your snake under the desk ?
mouse
frog
behind
in front of
wastepaper basket
shoe
pot plant
Yes, it is.
No, it isn't.

8 Biology Quiz

Work in pairs (A, B).
Step 1: A fills in grid A, B fills in grid B.
Step 2: A looks at the empty B grid and asks B, for example:

Do monkeys eat . . .?

Yes, they do. (+)
No, they don't. (–)
I don't know. (?)

Step 3: B looks at the empty A grid and asks A.
B fills in what A says.

A	nuts	rats	beetles	grass
monkeys	☐	☐	☐	☐
elephants	☐	☐	☐	☐
frogs	☐	☐	☐	☐
snakes	☐	☐	☐	☐
parrots	☐	☐	☐	☐

B	bananas	honey	caterpillars	eggs
monkeys	☐	☐	☐	☐
elephants	☐	☐	☐	☐
frogs	☐	☐	☐	☐
snakes	☐	☐	☐	☐
parrots	☐	☐	☐	☐

9

Listen to the cassette and check your grids.
Then write down what the animals eat.

Example:
Parrots eat . . .
They don't eat . . .

10 A song

Come, let's sing the alphabet

Come, let's sing the alphabet.
Come, let's sing the alphabet.
A, b, c, d, e, f, g,
come to the circus with me.
A, b, c, d, e, f, g,
come to the circus with me.
H, i, j, k, l, m, n, o,
let's go and see the circus show.
H, i, j, k, l, m, n, o,
let's go and see the circus show.
P, q, r, s, t, u, v,
come and have some fun with me.
P, q, r, s, t, u, v,
come and have some fun with me.
W, x, y and z,
let's all sing the alphabet.
Let's all sing the alphabet.

a	[eɪ]	n	[en]
b	[biː]	o	[əʊ]
c	[siː]	p	[piː]
d	[diː]	q	[kjuː]
e	[iː]	r	[ɑː]
f	[ef]	s	[es]
g	[dʒiː]	t	[tiː]
h	[eɪtʃ]	u	[juː]
i	[aɪ]	v	[viː]
j	[dʒeɪ]	w	['dʌbljuː]
k	[keɪ]	x	[eks]
l	[el]	y	[waɪ]
m	[em]	z	[zed]

Study and change

Read the texts below. Close your eyes.
Imagine your crazy picture of the circus director's caravan.
Write a text and then draw your picture.

Text 1

Joe Blue is a circus director.
In his caravan the snake is in
the wastepaper basket. The frog is
on the desk. The elephant is
in the cupboard and the mouse is
on the curtain.

Text 2

Come and see the circus director's
caravan. The elephant is behind
the curtain. The mouse is in the shoe.
The snake is behind the pot plant.
The monkey is under the chair and
the frog is on the cupboard.
The circus director is
in the wastepaper basket and
the parrot is on the chair.

Grammar

Prepositions

How to ask where something is:

Where's the snake?
Where are Tom and Peter?

How to say where something is:

It's **behind** the caravan.
They're **in** the caravan.

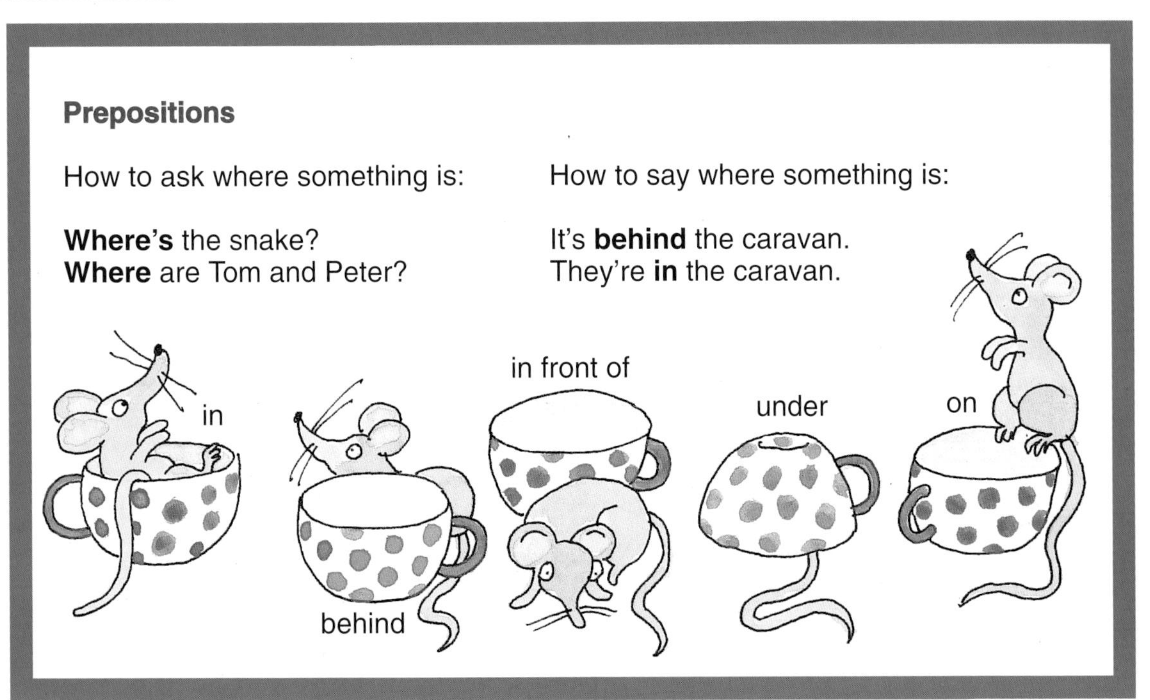

UNIT 7

MY BODY

1 Picture dictionary

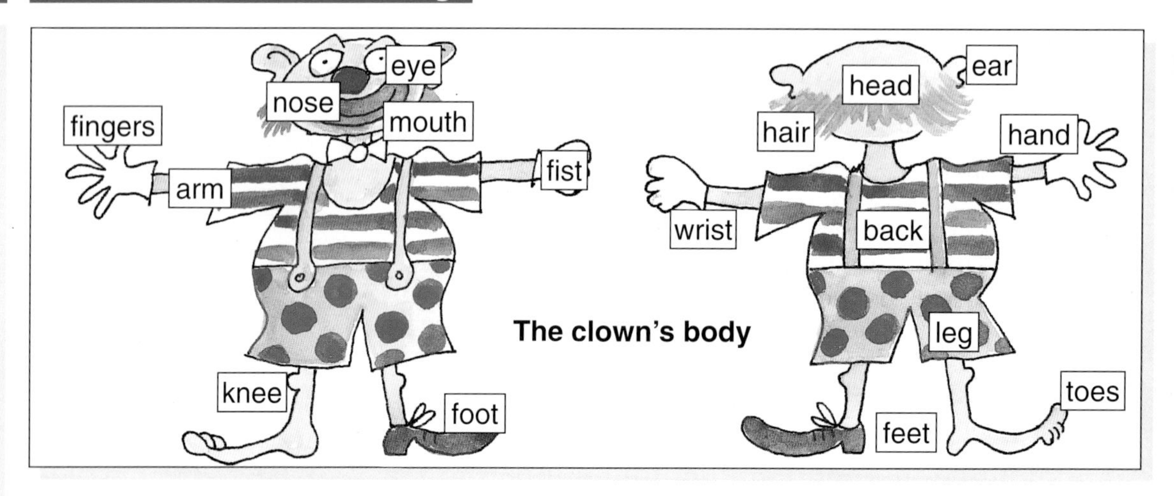

The clown's body

2

Work with a partner.
You point to a part of your body.
Your partner says the word.

3 A song

Listen to the song. Number the pictures from 1 to 12.
Then sing the song and do the actions.

The body song

I can
shake my fingers, make a fist,
shake my leg, touch my wrist.
Fingers, fist, leg, wrist!

I can
touch my knees, touch my toes,
close my eyes, touch my nose.
Knees, toes, eyes, nose!

I can
shake my head, stamp my feet,
touch my hair and – take a seat!
Head, feet, take a seat!

4

Listen to the dialogues. ✔ Tick the correct answers.

Dialogue 1

The boy's hands hurt. ☐
The boy's knee hurts. ☐
The boy's wrist hurts. ☐

Dialogue 2

The girl's feet hurt. ☐
The girl's nose hurts. ☐
The girl's back hurts. ☐

Dialogue 3

The boy's finger hurts. ☐
The boy's toes hurt. ☐
The boy's head hurts. ☐

Dialogue 4

The girl's ears hurt. ☐
The girl's mouth hurts. ☐
The girl's eye hurts. ☐

NOTE
I've got **a** headache.
But:
I've got toothache.
I've got stomachache.

5 A sketch

Listen. Then act out the sketch.

Hi, Simon. How are you today?
Not very well. I've got a headache.

Hallo, Simon. How are you?
Oh, not very well. I've got toothache.

Hi, Simon. Are you alright?
No, I'm not very well. My knee hurts.

Hey, Simon! Let's go to the circus.
No, I can't. I've got a cold.

Simon, let's go to David's party.
No, I can't. I've got a headache, I've got toothache, my knee hurts, I've got a cold and I've got stomachache.

But Susan's at the party!
What?! Oh, I think I'm OK!

6 Melanie likes the book "Stanley, the lolly monster".

Listen to Melanie and Brian.  *Tick true (T) or false (F).*

	T	F
The lolly monster eats lots of lollies.		
He's got a blue and pink body.		
His head is blue and his hair is yellow.		
He's got five legs.		
He's got twenty-five toes.		
His arms are yellow and orange.		
He's got three red eyes and a big blue nose.		
His ears are small and blue.		
His mouth is big and green.		

Now talk about Stanley, the lolly monster.
Make the false sentences true.

He hasn't got a . . . He's got . . .
His head isn't . . . His head is . . .

7 *Read the text about Georgina, the toffee monster.*
Look at the drawing and make the false sentences true.

She hasn't got six . . . She's got . . .
Her body isn't . . . Her body is . . .

This is Georgina, the toffee monster. Georgina eats lots of toffees. Her body is white and pink. She has got six legs and four arms. Her head is yellow and her hair is blue. Her big eyes are blue. She has got a big red mouth. Her arms are green and her hands are orange.

8 Grammar rhythm

Listen to the grammar rhythm and fill in the words from the box.

my your his her its our your their

I – my
you – ________
he – ________
she – ________
it – ________
we – ________
you – ________
they – ________

Can you shake ________ fingers, make a fist,
shake ________ leg, touch ________ wrist?
Fingers, fist, leg, wrist!

I can
shake ________ fingers, make a fist,
shake ________ leg, touch ________ wrist.
Fingers, fist, leg, wrist!

Look at Martin.
He can
touch ________ knees, touch ________ toes,
close ________ eyes, touch ________ nose.
Knees, toes, eyes, nose!

And now look at Cindy.
She can shake ________ head, stamp ________ feet,
touch ________ hair and – take a seat.
Head, feet, take a seat.

And now look at the snake.
Can it shake ________ fingers,
stamp ________ feet,
touch ________ nose or touch ________ toe?
No, no, no.

Hey you, kids!
Can you shake ________ fingers, make fists,
shake ________ legs and touch ________ wrists?
Fingers, fists, legs, wrists.

We can shake ________ fingers, make fists,
shake ________ legs, touch ________ wrists.
Fingers, fists, legs, wrists!

Look at Martin and Cindy.
They can touch ________ knees, touch ________ toes,
close their eyes, touch ________ nose.
Knees, toes, eyes, nose!

Pronunciation

Listen to the words and repeat them.
Then listen again and tick ✔ the sound you hear.

	[k]	[s]	[z]
kid	☐	☐	☐
face	☐	☐	☐
toes	☐	☐	☐
caravan	☐	☐	☐
circus	☐	☐	☐

	[k]	[s]	[z]
blazer	☐	☐	☐
class	☐	☐	☐
has	☐	☐	☐
house	☐	☐	☐
blouse	☐	☐	☐

Study and change

Study the text about Georgina, the toffee monster, in **7**. *Then write a text about George, the ice-cream monster, or Wilma, the chocolate monster, and draw a picture.*

Grammar

Possessive Pronouns

How to say that something belongs to somebody:

UNIT 8

1

Listen to the cassette.
Write in the days of the week.

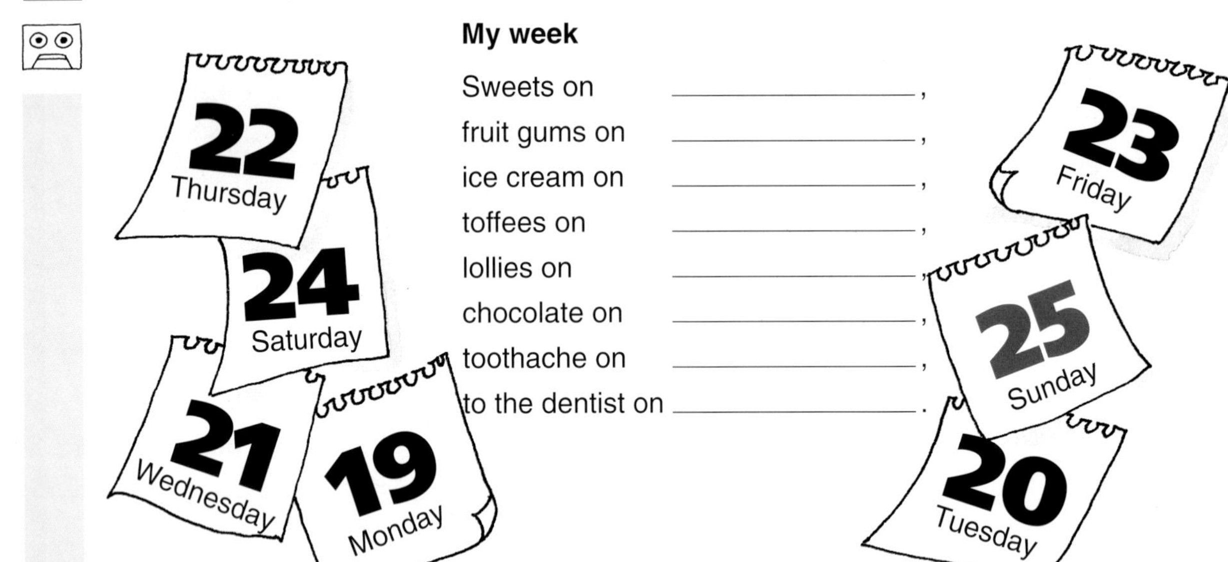

My week

Sweets on ____________,
fruit gums on ____________,
ice cream on ____________,
toffees on ____________,
lollies on ____________,
chocolate on ____________,
toothache on ____________,
to the dentist on ____________.

2

Ask your teacher for the meaning of the words in the box.

What's "..." in your language?

angry bad luck a bad day duck look at smile

3 A story

Read the story.

Bad luck for Arnold

Arnold Croc, the crocodile, eats parrots, ducks and cats. He doesn't like apples, bananas or oranges. He eats monkeys, snakes and frogs. He doesn't like chocolate, fruit gums or popcorn. Arnold Croc makes a plan for the week. He writes a list.

Here is Arnold's list:

Arnold Croc, the crocodile, looks at the list and smiles.
Monday is a bad day for Arnold. He has a cold. No parrot for Arnold.
On Tuesday Arnold has a headache. No duck for Arnold.
On Wednesday Arnold's knee hurts. No cat for Arnold.
On Thursday and Friday Arnold has toothache. No monkey and no snake for Arnold.
On Saturday the frog jumps on Arnold's back. "Where's the frog?" Arnold says. He is very angry. And he is very, very hungry.
On Sunday Arnold goes to the banana tree. He eats and eats and eats. Then he has stomachache.

4 *Make sentences.*

On Monday	his knee hurts.
On Tuesday	Arnold eats and eats and eats.
On Wednesday	he has a headache.
On Thursday and Friday	the frog jumps on Arnold's back.
On Saturday	Arnold has a cold.
On Sunday	he has toothache.

5 *Now listen to the story.*
How many sentences about Arnold can you make?

Arnold likes . . .	He doesn't like . . .
He eats . . .	He doesn't eat . . .
He makes a . . .	He writes a . . .
He looks at . . .	He has a . . .
He goes to the . . .	He has . . .

Work with a partner. Can you guess the picture puzzle? Then listen to the cassette and check.

On M ________ Mickey, the ________, ________ 10 ________.

On T ________ h__ ________ 20 f____ g ____ ________

On W________ h__ ________ 30 ________.

On T________ + F________ h__ ________ 40 ________

On S________ h__ ________ 50 t ________.

On S________ Mickey ________.

He i__ i___

H___ h___ a________

7 A song

Bad luck for Arnold

Bad luck for Arnold, ooh ooh.
That's bad luck for Arnold, ooh ooh.

Arnold doesn't like bananas,
he eats parrots.
Arnold doesn't like bananas,
he eats ducks and cats.
Arnold doesn't like bananas,
he eats monkeys, snakes and frogs.
Arnold doesn't like bananas.
That's bad luck for Arnold, ooh ooh.
Yes, bad luck for Arnold, ooh ooh.

On Monday Arnold has a cold.
No parrot for Arnold.
On Tuesday Arnold has a headache.
No duck for Arnold.
On Wednesday Arnold's knee hurts.
No cat for Arnold. No, no, no.
On Thursday and Friday he has toothache.
No monkey and no snake.
And on Saturday the frog jumps on Arnold's back.
That's bad luck for Arnold, ooh ooh.
Yes, bad luck for Arnold, ooh ooh.

On Sunday Arnold is very hungry,
so he goes to the banana tree, ooh ooh.
He eats and eats and eats bananas,
and then he has stomachache, aarh!

Arnold doesn't like bananas.
That's bad luck for Arnold, ooh ooh.
Ooh, bad luck for Arnold, ooh ooh.
Yes, bad luck for Arnold, ooh ooh.
Mmmmmh, bad luck for Arnold.

Pronunciation

Listen to the words on the cassette. Underline the words with the sound [æ] *as in cat* [kæt].

answer
black
man
woman
arm
alphabet
class
hand
happy
fast
apple
camera

Listen to the words on the cassette and ✔ tick the sound you hear.

	[ɪ]	[iː]
seat	☐	☐
meet	☐	☐
feet	☐	☐
fifty	☐	☐
beetle	☐	☐
see	☐	☐
fist	☐	☐
green	☐	☐

Study and change

Read the text about Pippa, the parrot.
Then write your own text about another animal.

On Monday Pippa eats twelve apples.
On Tuesday she eats twenty-two bananas.
On Wednesday she eats thirty-three strawberries.
On Thursday and Friday she eats forty-four oranges.
And on Saturday she eats fifty-five fruit gums.
On Sunday she is in bed. She has stomachache.

Grammar

like – don't like

How to say whether you like or don't liike something:

I **like** toffees, but I **don't like** lollies.
I **like** strawberry ice cream, but I **don't like** vanilla ice cream.

likes – doesn't like

How to say whether someone likes or doesn't like something:

Arnold **likes** ducks, but he **doesn't like** apples.
Arnold **likes** frogs, but he **doesn't like** popcorn.

He likes me, he doesn't like me, he....

Plurals

How to make the plural:

parrot
apple
toe
boy
monkey

parrot**s**
apple**s**
toe**s**
boy**s**
monkey**s**

Singular + s

Notice the spelling of words ending in **y**. If there is a consonant before the **y**, the **y** changes to **ies** in the plural.

lolly
strawberry
story

loll**ies**
strawberr**ies**
stor**ies**

Singular: y –› Plural: ies

If a word ends in **ch**, **x**, **s** or **sh**, add **es** for the plural.

toothbrush
class
box
inch

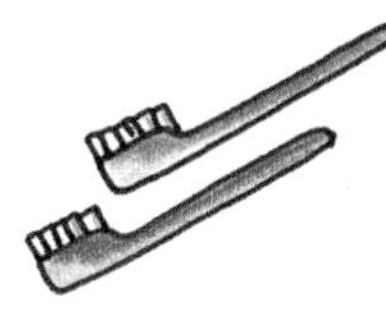

toothbrush**es**
class**es**
box**es**
inch**es**

Singular + es

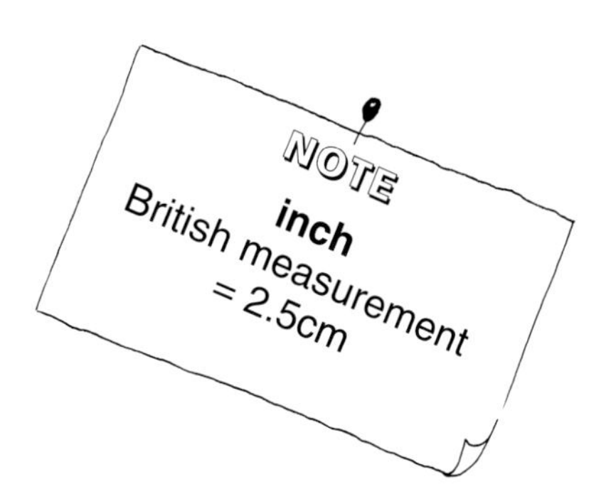

UNIT 9

What's the time?

1 Picture dictionary

It's five o'clock.
It's five past five.
It's ten past five.
It's quarter past five.
It's twenty past five.
It's twenty-five past five.
It's half past five.
It's twenty-five to six.
It's twenty to six.
It's quarter to six.
It's ten to six.
It's five to six.

2 *Look at the watches and clocks. Read out the times. Then listen to the cassette. ✔ Tick true or false.*

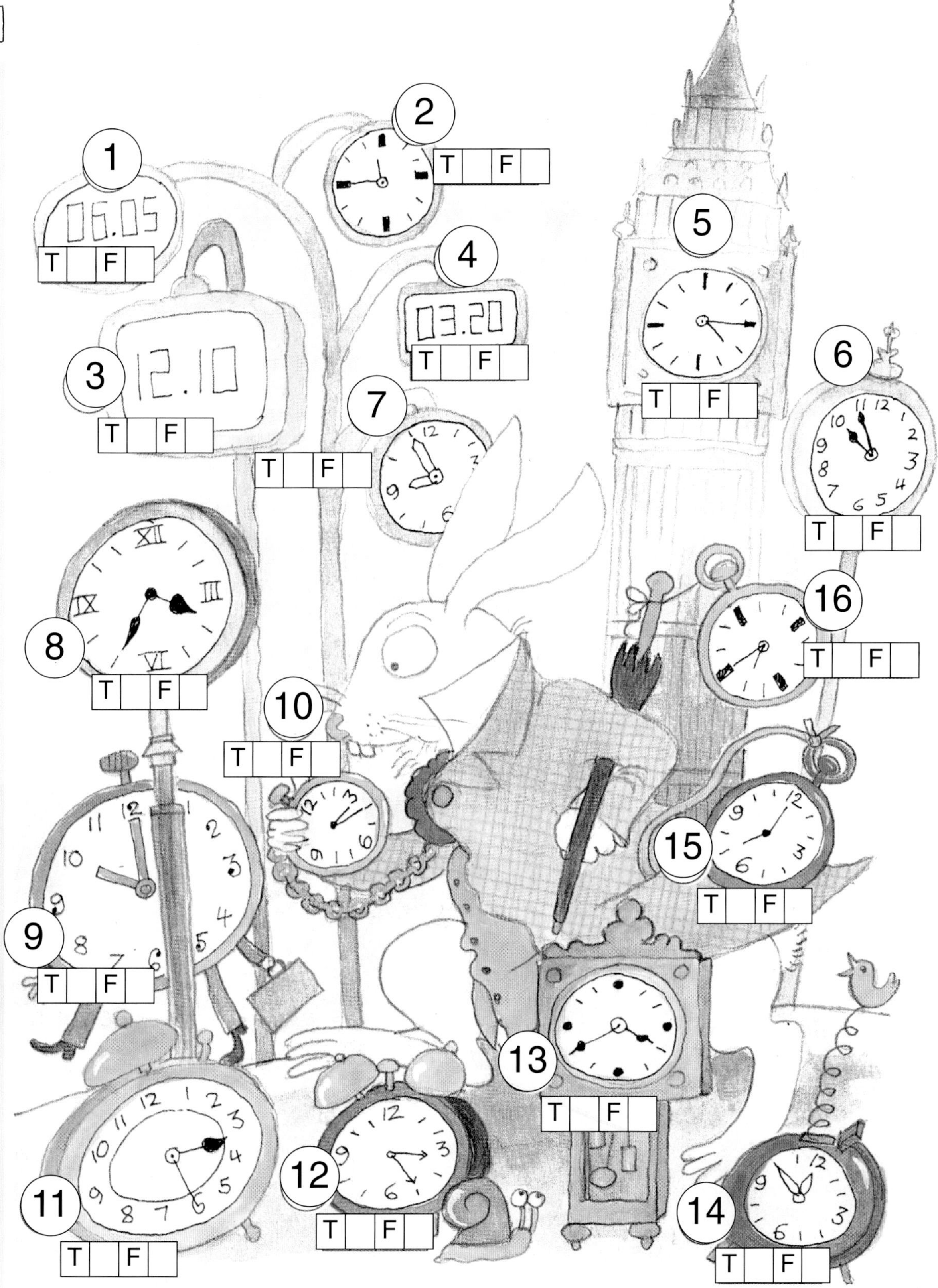

3 Anna's day

Look at the pictures. Listen to the cassette. Fill in the times.

get up/

____________ o'clock

have breakfast/
at half

____

go to school/
at ten past

____

school starts/
at quarter

____

school ends/

____________ o'clock

get home/

____

to five

Then do home work

or play with friends

or watch TV

go to bed/at quarter past

____

4

Make sentences about Anna.

Anna gets up at . . .

She has . . .

She goes to . . .

School starts at . . .

School ends at . . .

She . . .

Then she . . .

. . .

5

Make sentences about yourself.

I get up at . . .

I go to school at . . .

I get home at . . .

Then I . . .

I go to bed at . . .

6

Look at the watches and fill in the correct letters.

NOTE
am = after midnight until 12 o'clock midday
pm = after 12 o'clock midday until midnight

◯ It's nine twenty-five pm.

◯ It's seven forty pm.

◯ It's eleven am.

◯ It's five thirty pm.

◯ It's five thirty am.

◯ It's eleven pm.

◯ It's nine twenty-five am.

◯ It's seven forty am.

7

Look at the time zones. It's 12 am in London.
Draw the correct times for the other cities on the clocks.
Then say what time it is in the other cities.

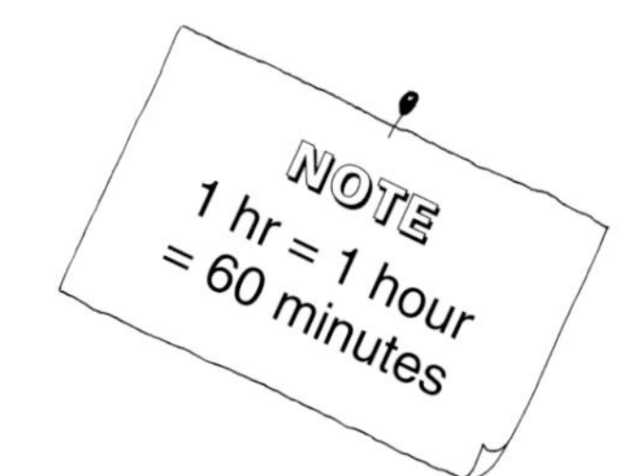

In Moscow it's one pm . . .
In New York . . .

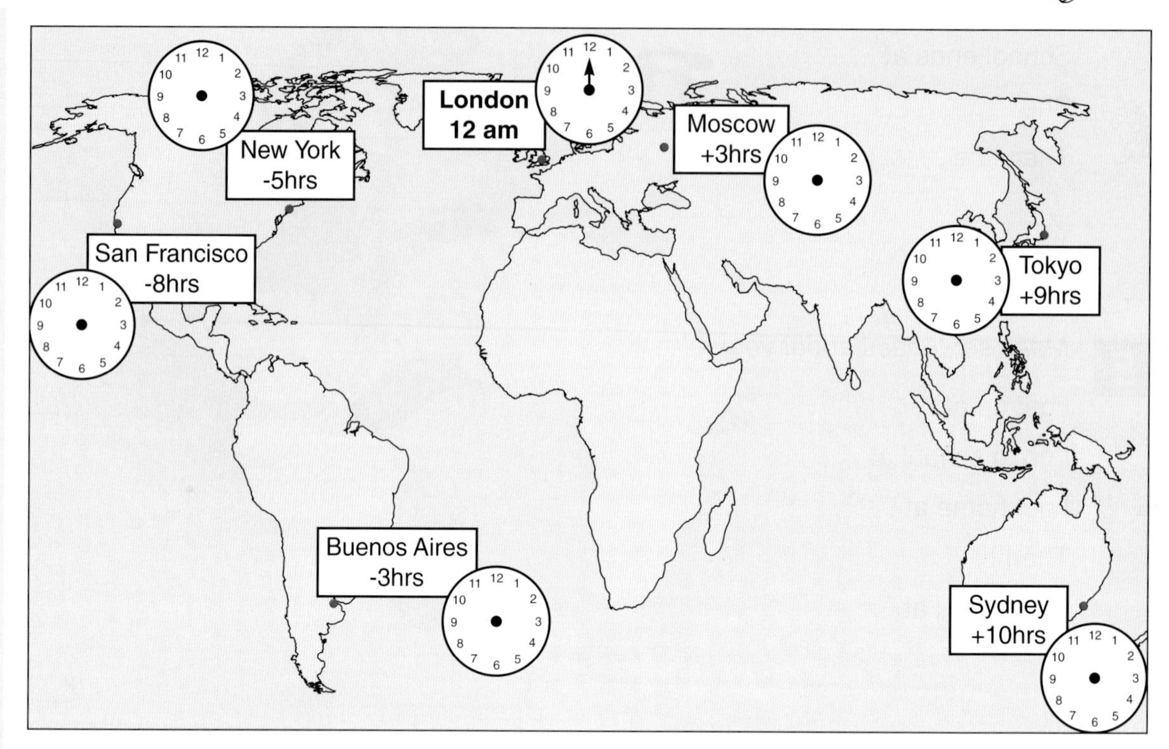

8

Get together with a partner.
Ask your partner questions like this:

It's half past nine am in Moscow.
What's the time in New York?

It's half past one am.

Study and change

Read this text by an English schoolgirl.
Then write a text about your day or your friend's day.

I get up at half past seven and I have breakfast at quarter to eight.
I go to school at quarter past eight. School starts at nine o'clock and ends at four o'clock. I get home at five o'clock. Then I do my homework, watch TV or play with my friends. I go to bed at nine o'clock.

Grammar

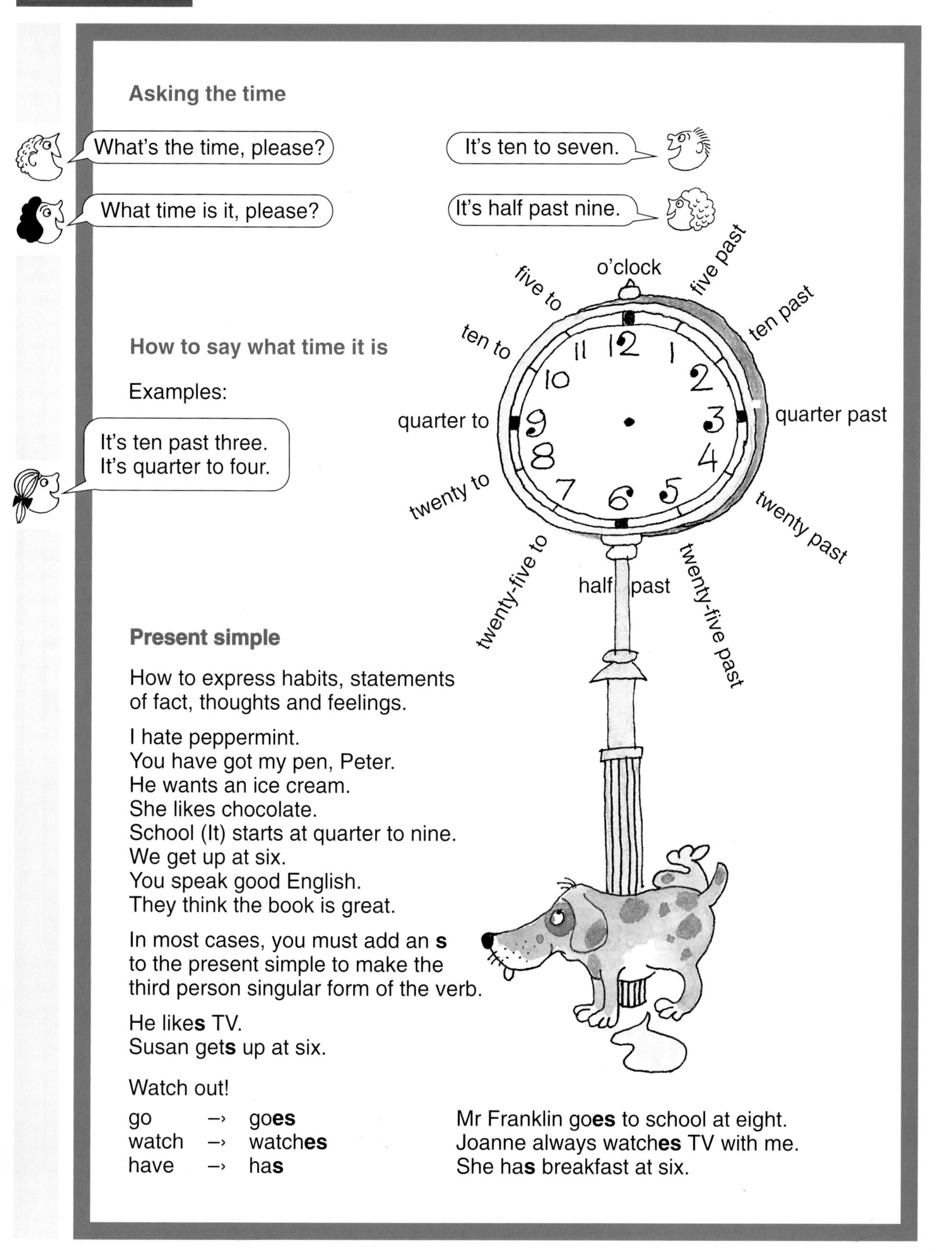

Asking the time

What's the time, please?

It's ten to seven.

What time is it, please?

It's half past nine.

How to say what time it is

Examples:

It's ten past three.
It's quarter to four.

Present simple

How to express habits, statements of fact, thoughts and feelings.

I hate peppermint.
You have got my pen, Peter.
He wants an ice cream.
She likes chocolate.
School (It) starts at quarter to nine.
We get up at six.
You speak good English.
They think the book is great.

In most cases, you must add an **s** to the present simple to make the third person singular form of the verb.

He like**s** TV.
Susan get**s** up at six.

Watch out!

go –› go**es**
watch –› watch**es**
have –› ha**s**

Mr Franklin go**es** to school at eight.
Joanne always watch**es** TV with me.
She ha**s** breakfast at six.

UNIT 10

That's me!

1 Picture dictionary

swim

run

sing

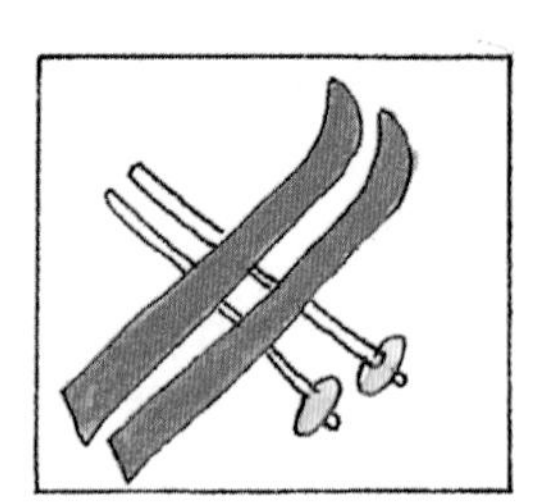

ski

play football

climb trees

juggle

ride a bike

play volleyball

dance

ride a horse

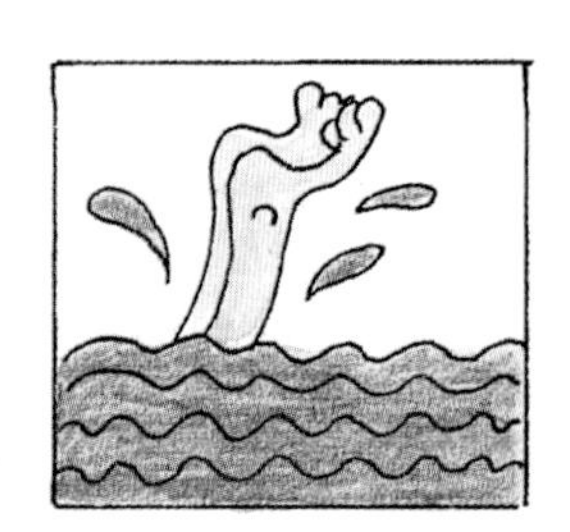

dive

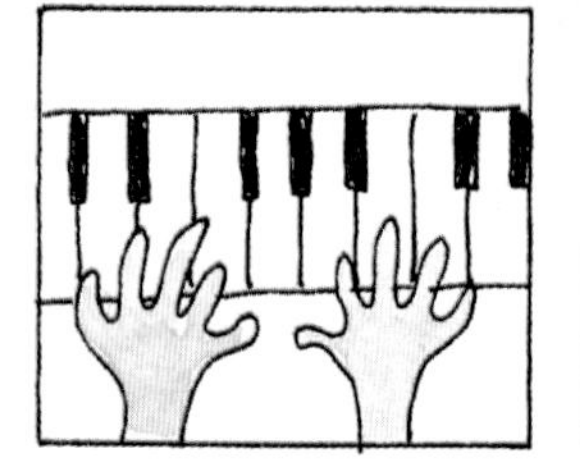

play the piano

play the guitar

play the recorder

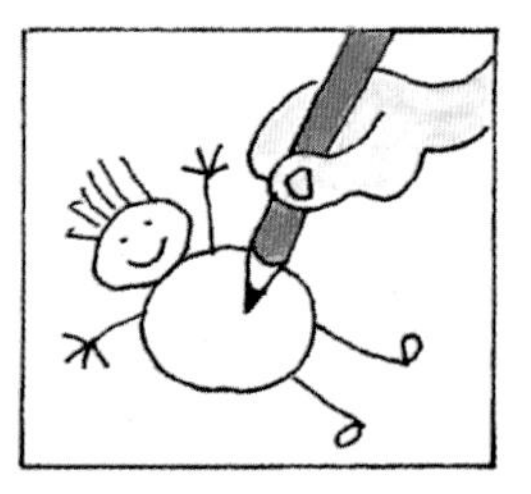

draw

2 Grammar rhythm

Listen and fill in the words.

swimming
singing
juggling
skiing

Can you ski?

Can you ski?
Yes, I can,
I'm good at ___________________.
Can you swim?
Yes, I can,
I'm good at ___________________.
Can you juggle?
Yes, I can,
I'm good at ___________________.
Can you sing?
Yes, I can,
I'm good at ___________________.
So, you can ski and swim and juggle and sing?
Yes, I can,
I'm good at ___________________ and ___________________
and ___________________ and ___________________.
But can you tell the truth?
No.

3

Talk about yourself.

I can swim .

I can't juggle .

I'm good at skiing .

I'm not good at singing .

I can ... , but I can't ... .

I'm good at ... ing, but I'm not good at ... ing.

...but I'm good at singing

4 *Talk to a partner.*

Can you . . .?
Yes, I can.
No, I can't.
Are you good at . . .ing?
Yes, I am.
No, I'm not.
NOTE
I cannot = I can't
I am = I'm
I am not = I'm not

5 *Look at the words in the box.*
Ask your teacher.

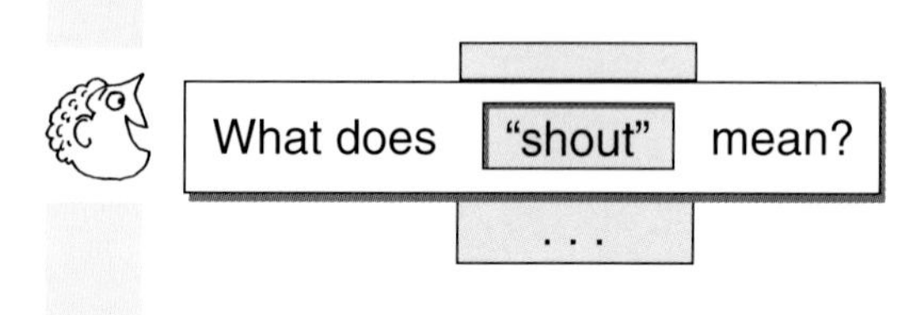
What does "shout" mean?
. . .

shout	smile	nothing	laugh	go away	go back
teach	help	seal	blackbird	at this moment	

6 A story

Read the story.

Percy, the penguin

One day Percy, the penguin, meets his two friends: Peter, the bear, and Matilda, the blackbird.
"Percy, can you climb trees?" Peter, the bear, says.
"No, I can't," Percy says. The bear laughs and climbs a tree.
"Percy, can you sing?" Matilda, the blackbird, says.
"No, I can't," Percy says. Matilda laughs and sings a beautiful song.
"Look," Percy says, "I can swim."
He jumps into the water and swims.
"Phew, that's nothing," Peter and Matilda say.
Percy is sad. He goes away. He comes to a circus. He meets a seal. The seal is juggling.
"Fantastic," Percy says, "please teach me to juggle."
"Okay," the seal says. The seal teaches Percy to juggle. Percy is happy. Now he can juggle.
He goes back to his friends.
"Look," he says to Matilda and Peter.
"I can juggle."
"Phew, that's nothing," his friends say.

Percy is very sad. He turns round. At that moment a baby bird falls into the water. It cannot swim.
"Help, help!" it shouts.
"Help, help!" Matilda and Peter shout.
Percy jumps into the water and helps the baby bird out.
"Oh, thank you, thank you, Percy," the baby bird says.
"Fantastic, Percy," Matilda and Peter say.
Peter and Matilda look at Percy.
"Please teach us to swim," they say.
"And please teach us to juggle."
Percy looks at his friends and smiles.

7

True or false?

- ☐ Percy has two friends: Peter, the cat, and Matilda, the blackbird.
- ☐ Percy is good at climbing trees.
- ☐ Matilda is good at singing.
- ☐ In the circus, Percy meets an elephant.
- ☐ The elephant teaches Percy to juggle.
- ☐ Percy juggles and his friends say: "Fantastic!"
- ☐ A baby bird falls into the water.
- ☐ The baby bird cannot swim.
- ☐ Matilda and Peter jump into the water and help the baby bird out.
- ☐ "Please teach us to juggle," Matilda and Peter say.

8

Listen to the story "Percy, the penguin" on cassette.
Then work in groups of five. Act out the story.
There are five roles: Percy, the penguin – Peter, the bear – Matilda, the blackbird – the seal – the baby bird.

Pronunciation

Listen to the words on the cassette and ✔ tick the sound you hear.

	[æ]	[e]	[eɪ]
end	☐	☐	☐
happy	☐	☐	☐
hand	☐	☐	☐
late	☐	☐	☐
back	☐	☐	☐
head	☐	☐	☐

	[æ]	[e]	[eɪ]
day	☐	☐	☐
ten	☐	☐	☐
bed	☐	☐	☐
sad	☐	☐	☐
sandwich	☐	☐	☐
snake	☐	☐	☐

Listen to the words on the cassette.
Underline the words with the sound [ʌ] *as in but* [bʌt].

hungry hundred put run super hurt monkey frog stomach touch

Study and change

Text 1

I am very good at skiing and running.
I am good at football.
I can swim, but I can't dive.
I am not very good at volleyball and I can't play tennis, ride a horse or juggle.

Text 2

I am very good at playing the piano and at singing. I can play the recorder, but I can't play the guitar.
I am good at dancing and I can juggle.
I can draw, but I am not very good at it.
I am not very good at sport.
I can't ride a horse and I can't dive, but I can swim.

Grammar

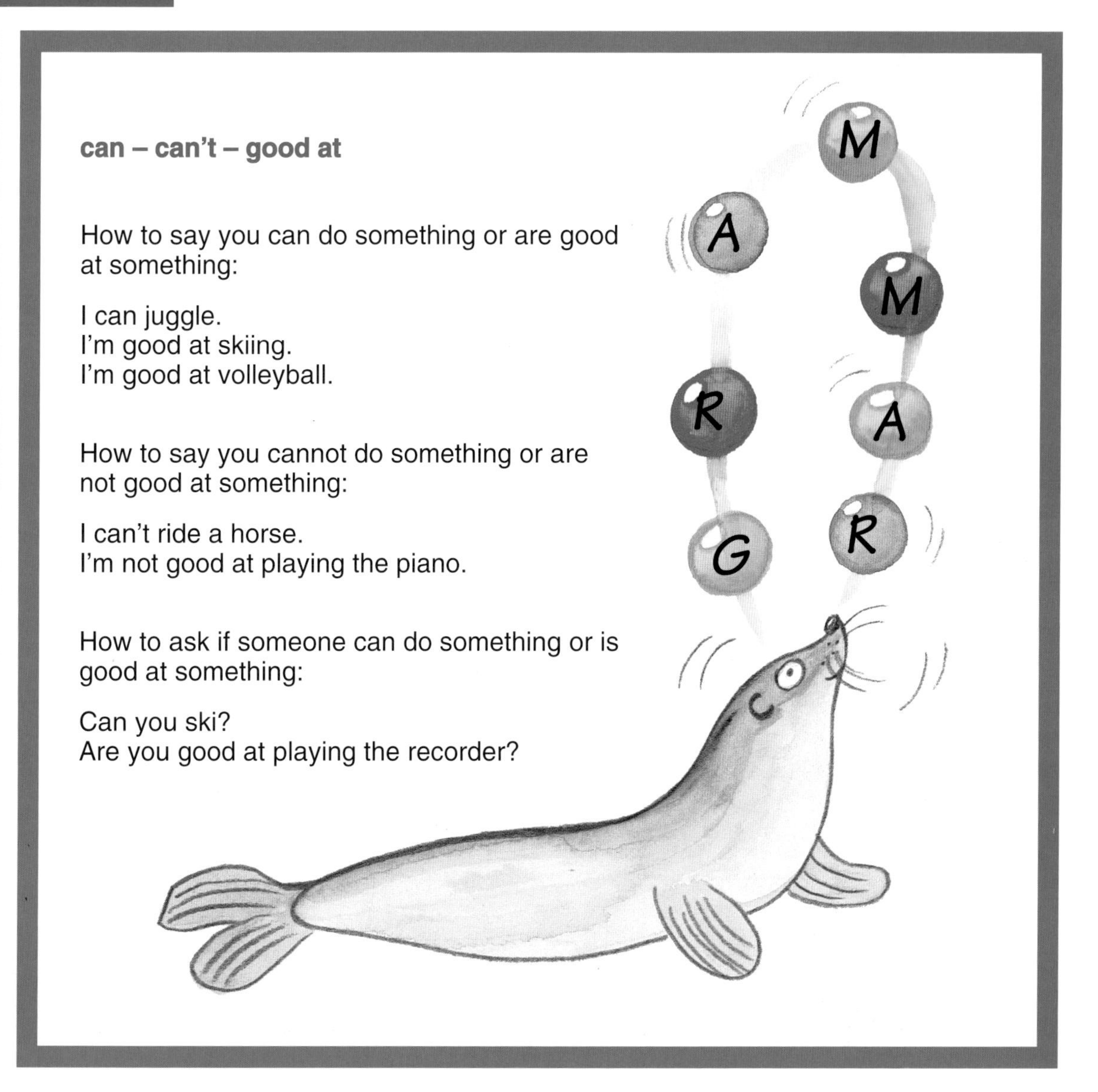

can – can't – good at

How to say you can do something or are good at something:

I can juggle.
I'm good at skiing.
I'm good at volleyball.

How to say you cannot do something or are not good at something:

I can't ride a horse.
I'm not good at playing the piano.

How to ask if someone can do something or is good at something:

Can you ski?
Are you good at playing the recorder?

UNIT 11

FOOD

1 Picture dictionary

2

Listen to these people ordering food in a fast-food restaurant. ✔ Tick the food they order, and write L (large), M (medium) or S (small) for the chips and drinks.

Menu	Man	Girl	Boy
hamburger			
doubleburger			
cheeseburger			
fishburger			
chickenburger			
chicken nuggets			
chips – large, small			
ketchup			
mustard			
coke – large, medium, small			
orange juice – large, medium, small			
strawberry milk shake – large, medium, small			

3 *Read through the dialogue and then listen to it on cassette.*
Then act it out in groups of three.

In a fast-food restaurant

Man:	Next, please.
Sheila:	What do you want, John?
John:	A doubleburger and chips.
Sheila:	Two doubleburgers and chips, please.
Man:	Small or large chips?
Sheila:	John?
John:	Large.
Sheila:	One small, one large, please.
Man:	With mustard?
Sheila and John:	Yes, please.
Man:	Anything else?
Sheila:	Two cokes, please.
Man:	Large, medium or small?
Sheila and John:	Medium.
Man:	That's £7.40.
Sheila:	Oh, I haven't got my money with me.
John:	I've got no money.
Man:	Oh no! Next, please! Next, please!

4 *Work with a partner. Munchie and Crunchie love eating and drinking. Partner A picks Munchie's seven favourite things from the picture dictionary, and writes them on a piece of paper. Partner B does the same for Crunchie. You have fifteen guesses to find out what these things are.*

Ask questions like this:

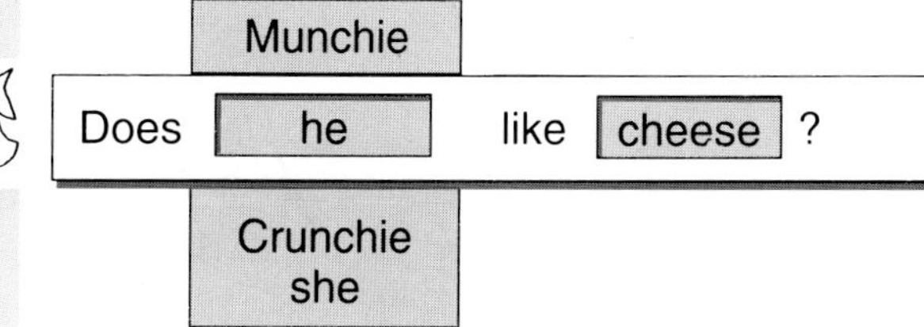

	Munchie		
Does	he	like	cheese ?
	Crunchie she		

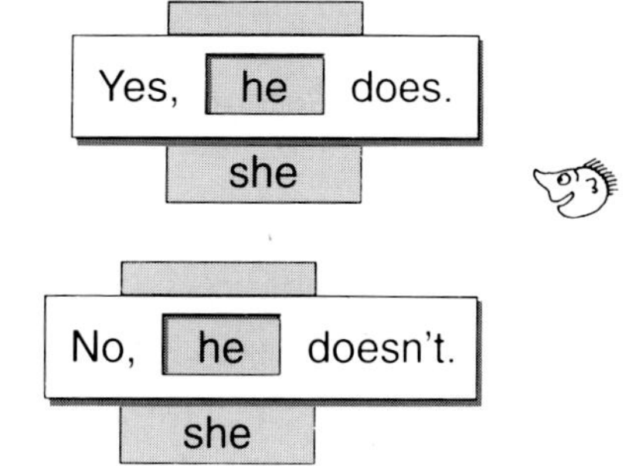

Yes,	he she	does.
No,	he she	doesn't.

5

Find somebody who . . .
Look at the list below. Walk around in class.
Ask your classmates:

What's your favourite vegetable?
What vegetable do you hate?

Write their names in the boxes.

	FAVOURITE	HATE
carrots		
cabbage		
peas		
potatoes		
tomatoes		
spinach		
beans		

NOTE
potato potato**es**
tomato tomato**es**

6

Work in pairs. Fill in the list.
Ask your partner about your teacher:

What do you think?
Does he/she like . . .?

✔ *Tick the answerboxes.*
Then your teacher says what he/she likes.
Count your partner's correct guesses.

My teacher's name:

____

What my partner thinks:	☺	☹
spinach		
tomatoes		
cabbage		
fishburgers		
chicken nuggets		
ketchup		
chips		
chewing gum		
chocolate		
ice cream		

No, I don't like chewing gum.

7 Grammar rhythm

Listen to the grammar rhythm.
Then do it in class.

Munchie and Crunchie

Does Munchie like carrots?
No, he doesn't.
Does Munchie like cabbage?
No, he doesn't.
Does Munchie like peas?
No, he doesn't.
Does Munchie like spinach?
No, he doesn't.
What does Munchie like?
What does he like?
Tell me.

Munchie likes chicken,
and he likes cake.
Munchie likes chips
and strawberry shake.
Oh, yeah.

Does Crunchie like tomatoes?
No, she doesn't.
Does Crunchie like beans?
No, she doesn't.
Does Crunchie like potatoes?
No, she doesn't.
Does Crunchie like juice?
No, she doesn't.
What does Crunchie like?
What does she like?
Tell me, baby.

Crunchie likes coke.
Crunchie likes peas.
Crunchie likes ketchup,
and she likes cheese.
Oh, yeah.

Pronunciation

Listen to the words on the cassette and ✔ tick the sound you hear.

	[θ]	[ð]
mouth	☐	☐
truth	☐	☐
nothing	☐	☐
with	☐	☐
mother	☐	☐

	[θ]	[ð]
think	☐	☐
there	☐	☐
this	☐	☐
toothache	☐	☐
Thursday	☐	☐

Study and change

Text 1

My favourite food is spaghetti and my favourite drink is orange juice.
I also like sweets and ice cream.
I do not like tomatoes, but I like apples and strawberries.
I really hate cabbage.

Text 2

I like fishburgers with mustard and ketchup and orange juice.
I also like chicken nuggets, but I do not like sweet things. I do not like ice cream or toffees or chocolate.
On Sundays my mother makes hamburgers with peas, carrots and potatoes. That's my favourite food.

Grammar

do – does

How to ask questions with "do" and "does":

Do [you / they] like spinach?

Does [she / he] eat chips?

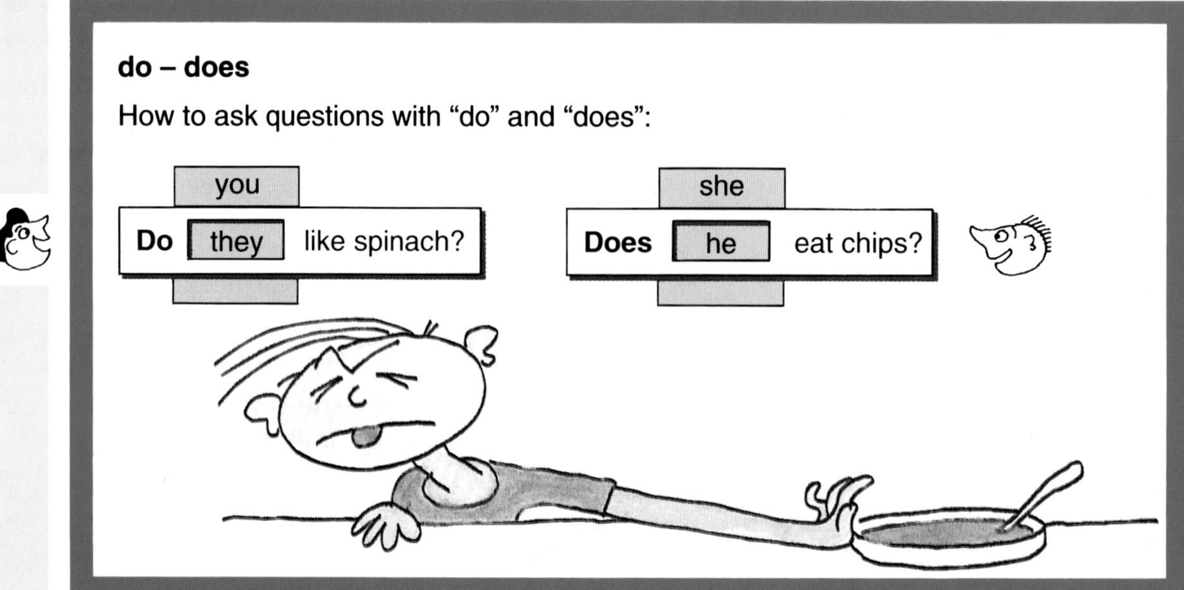

UNIT 12

Collecting things

1 *Write the numbers next to each word.*

- ◯ autographs
- ◯ badges
- ◯ comics
- ◯ coins
- ◯ postcards
- ◯ stickers
- ◯ stamps
- ◯ phonecards

2 *Work in groups of six. Find out what your classmates collect and report back.*

What do you collect?
Stamps.
Coins.
I don't collect things.
How many have you got?
Twenty.
About two hundred.
Example:
Two in our group collect stamps, two collect coins, one collects stickers, and one doesn't collect things.

3

Match the names of the countries to the map.

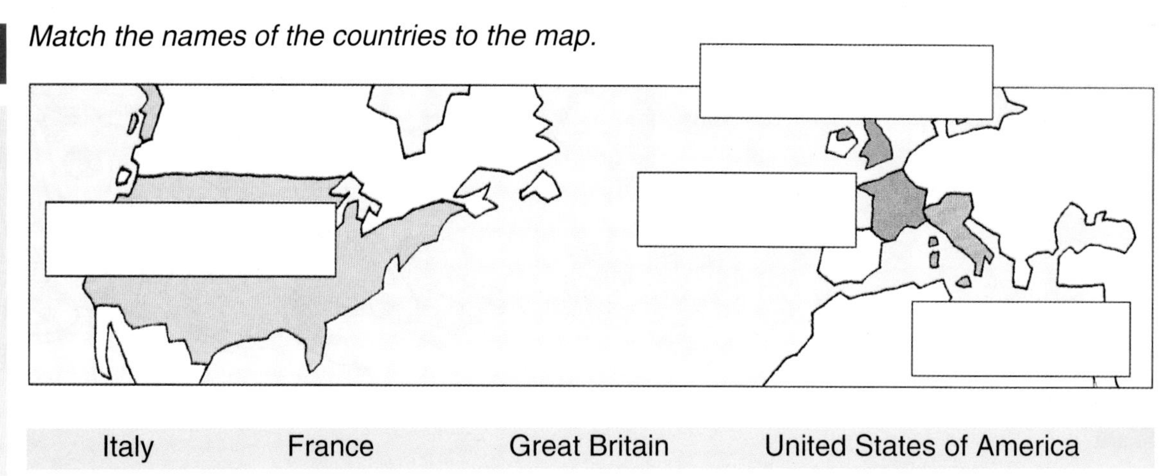

Italy	France	Great Britain	United States of America

Match the nationalities to the stamps.

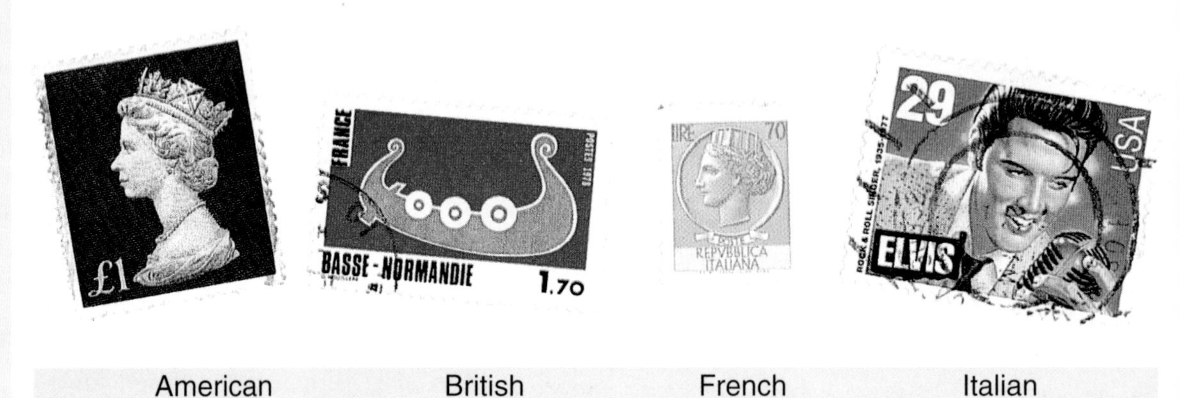

American	British	French	Italian

4

Listen to some British children. What do they collect?
How many things have they got? Mark the correct answers.

	Names	What?	How many?
Situation 1	Tracy	stickers badges comics	13 30 32
	David	badges stickers coins	16 46 64
Situation 2	Sheila	phonecards postcards comics	94 40 64
	Andy	phonecards postcards comics	100 150 200

	Names	What?	How many?
Situation 3	Mark	stickers postcards autographs	7 17 70
	Vicky	Italian stamps American stamps British stamps	about 200 about 500 about 800

5 A song

Look at the pictures and words in the box. Listen to the song and fill in the missing words.

The swapping song

Chorus:

Swap, swap, swap.
Let's do a swap.
Yeah, I like swapping.

Give me a ________________,
I'll give you a ________________.
Give me a ________________,
I'll give you a ________________.

Give me a ________________,
I'll give you a ________________.
Give me a ________________,
I'll give you a ________________.

(Chorus)

Give me a ________________,
I'll give you a ________________.
Give me a ________________,
I'll give you a ________________.

Give me the ________________,
I'll give you a ________________.
Give me a ________________,
I'll give you my ________________.

(Chorus)

6 The swapping game

Cut out the pictures on page 55 in your workbook.
Learn the language in the boxes below.
Then play the swapping game.
Your teacher will stop the game after a while.
Who is the winner? The boy or girl with the most things.

Have you got stamps?
No, I haven't.
Yes, I have.
How many have you got?
One.
Give me your stamp/ stamps/ . . . and I'll give you a . . ./ my . . .
OK, here you are.
No, I'm sorry.

7 Radio London

Learn through mime

Listen and look at the pictures.
Then close your books.
Listen again and mime the actions.

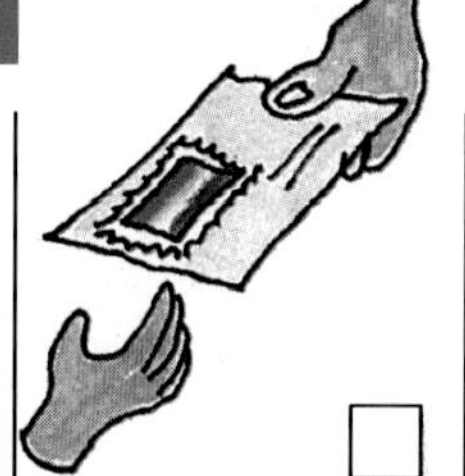

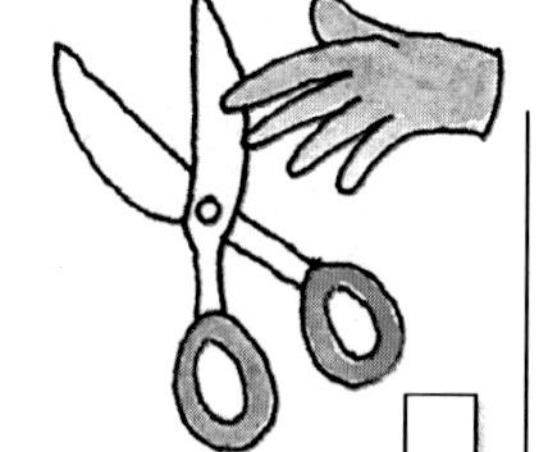

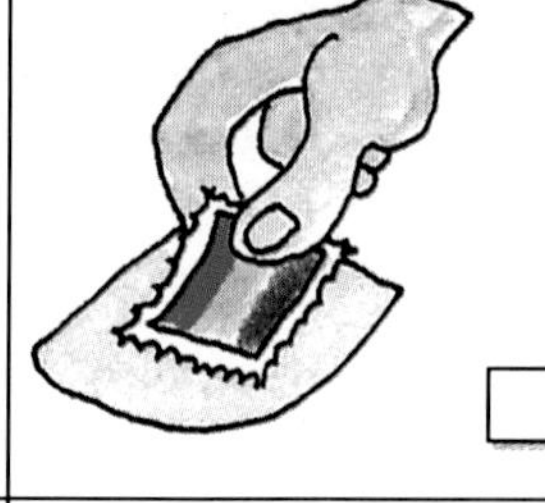

8

Take a pencil.
Listen and look at the pictures again.
Fill in the numbers.

9 A story

Listen to the story on the cassette. Nine words in the text below are wrong. They do not belong to the story. Underline them.

Generous George

George works for a farmer. The farmer gives him a horse. George is sad and gets on his horse to ride home. The sun is hot and he stops under a sofa. Suddenly he sees an old man with a dog. The old man looks very tired and is walking very slowly. "Take my horse and give me your pig," says George. So they swap phonecards. The old man is very happy and rides away on

the horse. Then a woman with a very old crocodile sits down under the tree. "I'm so happy," says the old woman. So George swaps his pig for the very old cat. Then he walks home. He is tired and hungry.
"Miaow," says the parrot. "Poor thing. You are hungry." So George goes out to catch a mouse for the hungry old cat. The cat goes with George. It stops in front of a mouse hole. George puts in his knee to catch a mouse for the cat. "But what's that?" George feels something hard. He pulls and pulls. It's a clock. He opens it. "What's that?" It is full of gold coins. George is happy. Now he can buy a lot of food for his old cat.

10 *Write down the words that are wrong.*
Then listen again and fill in the correct words.

WRONG	RIGHT
sad	happy
sofa	

Pronunciation

Listen to the words on the cassette and repeat them.
Then listen again and underline the odd one out in each line.

[əʊ]	postcard	phone	slow	story	photo
[ɔː]	more	four	pot	boring	door
[ɒ]	lolly	box	love	from	stop

Study and change

Text 1

I like collecting stickers.
I have got lots of stickers with pictures of animals and flowers. I have got about eighty or ninety. I collect American postcards too.
I have got postcards of New York, Florida and Texas.

Text 2

My friend Peter collects stamps.
I think he has got about three hundred.
He has got American, French, Italian, British and Austrian stamps. He collects stickers, phonecards and coins too.
He likes swapping stickers with me.
He swaps coins with our friends Anna and Alex. He does not like swapping stamps.

Grammar

lots of – a lot of

How to say that you have got a lot of stamps/stickers/etc:

I've got **lots of** stamps/stickers/comics.

I've got **a lot of** stamps/stickers/comics.

How many . . .?

Asking how many stamps/stickers/etc. someone has:

How many stamps/stickers/comics have you got?

ROOMS

1 Picture dictionary

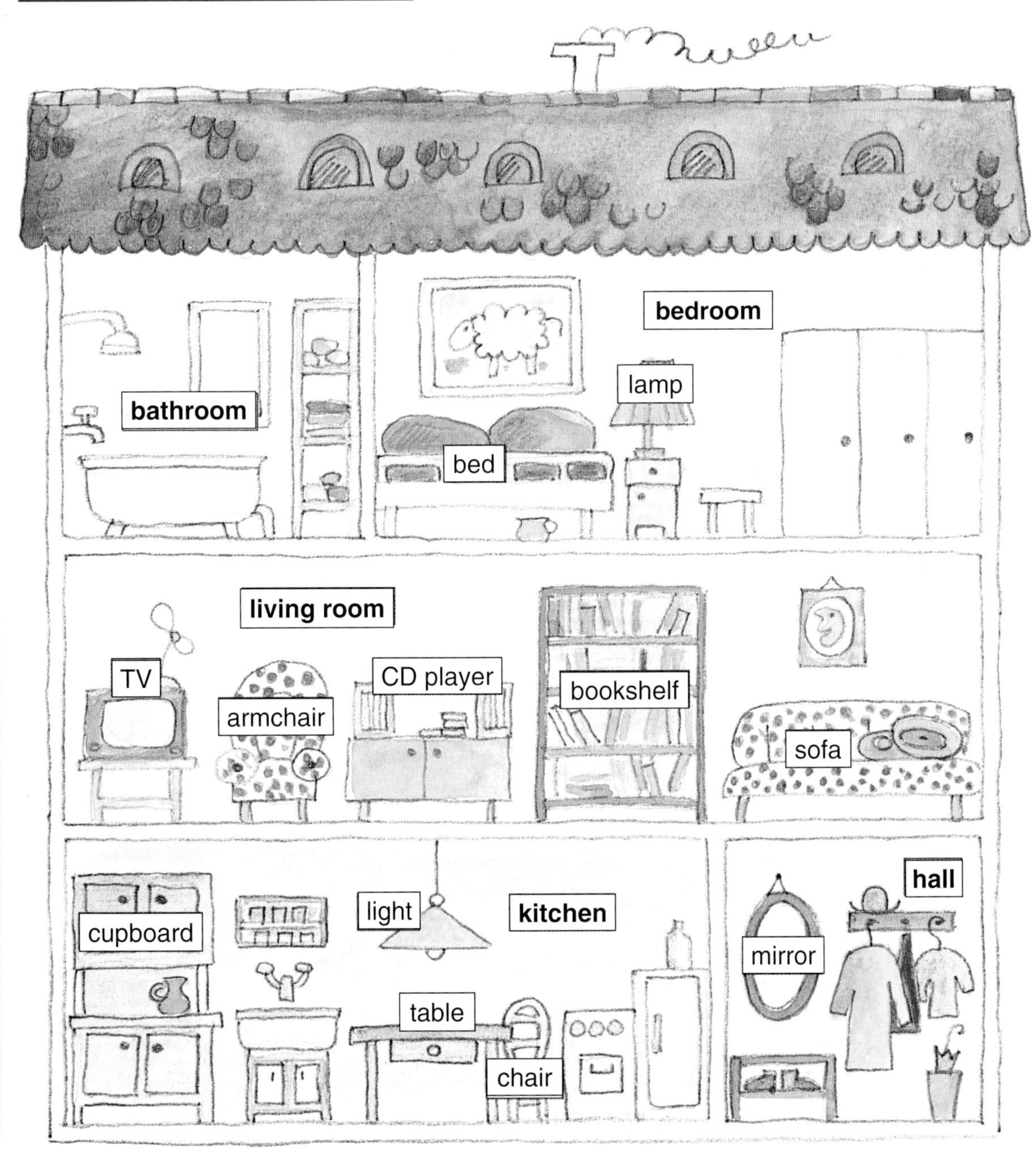

2

Listen to the cassette. Write the correct numbers in the pictures.

3

Listen to the cassette. Where are the noises coming from?
Who is making the noises? What is happening? ✔ Tick the correct answers.

UNIT 13

Situation 1

The noise is coming from the
- ☐ kitchen.
- ☐ bathroom.
- ☐ living room.
- ☐ bedroom.
- ☐ hall.

A
- ☐ man
- ☐ woman
- ☐ boy

is
- ☐ watching TV.
- ☐ sleeping.
- ☐ having a shower.
- ☐ cooking.
- ☐ opening the door.

Situation 2

The noise is coming from the
- ☐ kitchen.
- ☐ bathroom.
- ☐ living room.
- ☐ bedroom.
- ☐ hall.

A
- ☐ man
- ☐ woman
- ☐ girl

is
- ☐ watching TV.
- ☐ sleeping.
- ☐ having a shower.
- ☐ cooking.
- ☐ opening the door.

Situation 3

The noise is coming from the
- ☐ kitchen.
- ☐ bathroom.
- ☐ living room.
- ☐ bedroom.
- ☐ hall.

A
- ☐ man
- ☐ woman
- ☐ boy

is
- ☐ watching TV.
- ☐ sleeping.
- ☐ having a shower.
- ☐ cooking.
- ☐ opening the door.

Situation 4

The noise is coming from the
- ☐ kitchen.
- ☐ bathroom.
- ☐ living room.
- ☐ bedroom.
- ☐ hall.

A
- ☐ man
- ☐ woman
- ☐ boy

is
- ☐ watching TV.
- ☐ sleeping.
- ☐ having a shower.
- ☐ cooking.
- ☐ opening the door.

Situation 5

The noise is coming from the
- ☐ kitchen.
- ☐ bathroom.
- ☐ living room.
- ☐ bedroom.
- ☐ hall.

A
- ☐ man
- ☐ woman
- ☐ boy

is
- ☐ watching TV.
- ☐ sleeping.
- ☐ having a shower.
- ☐ cooking.
- ☐ opening the door.

4

Look at the picture of Carol's bedroom and read through the text. Underline the eight mistakes in the text.

In Carol's bedroom there is a window with red curtains. In front of the window there is a desk. Under the desk there is a computer. There is a wastepaper basket on the desk. There is a red bookshelf with a lot of books on it. There is a big poster of an elephant. The bed is pink. There is a very big mirror.

5

Talk about the mistakes in the text.

Example:

The curtains aren't red, they're blue.

The	...	isn't ..., it's ...	.
		aren't ..., they're ...	

There	isn't ...	, there is only	...	.
	aren't many ...			

6

Look at the pictures for one minute. Look at what the people are doing. Remember the actions. Then cover the pictures up.

7

Write in T (true) or F (false).

- ☐ In flat 1 a man is playing the piano.
- ☐ In flat 2 a girl is reading a book.
- ☐ In flat 3 a woman is dancing.
- ☐ In flat 4 a man and a woman are eating.
- ☐ In flat 5 a girl is drawing.
- ☐ In flat 6 a girl is playing the guitar.
- ☐ In flat 7 a boy is listening to music.
- ☐ In flat 8 a man is cooking.
- ☐ In flat 9 a boy is helping his father.

8

Look at the pictures in **6** *again.*
Make the false sentences true.

9

Listen to the dialogues. Complete the sentences with words from the box in the correct form.

watch a good film | eat | read a book | cook spaghetti | do homework

Situation 1	*Boy:*	Dad, can you help me with my homework?
	Dad:	Not now, I'm eating!
Situation 2	*Man:*	Darling, can you open the door?
	Woman:	No, I can't. ______
Situation 3	*Mum:*	Sylvia, can you go shopping for me?
	Sylvia:	Oh, mum, ______
Situation 4	*Mum:*	Peter! Time to go to bed.
	Peter:	But mum, ______
Situation 5	*Dad:*	John, can you come and help me in the garden?
	John:	Sorry, ______

10

Listen to the cassette again.
Act out the dialogues.

Sorry, Mum, I'm doing my homework

11 Grammar rhythm

Listen to the cassette and fill in the correct form of the verbs in the box.

NOTE
Elvis Presley: American rock 'n' roll singer (1935–1977)

clean
listen
eat
do
read
watch
help

No help for mum

Can you help me, Paul?
Oh mum, I'm ______________ my homework.

Can you help me, Gus?
Oh mum, I'm ______________ TV.

Can you help me, Dick?
Oh mum, I'm ______________ my bike.

Can you help me, Sue?
Oh mum, I'm ______________ my book.

Can you help me, Trish?
Oh mum, I'm ______________ to Elvis.

So you're ______________ your homework,
______________ TV,
______________ your bike,
______________ your book,
______________ to Elvis,
and you can't ______________ me
– ______________ the cake.

Study and change

Text 1

In my room there is a pink bed.
There are blue curtains and
a small desk. I have not got
a TV or a CD player.
On the shelf in my room
there are lots of books.
I have got a big poster
of a horse.

Text 2

Our living room is not very big. We have got
a green sofa and two green armchairs.
There is a small table in front of the sofa.
There are two windows with yellow and
green curtains. There is one lamp and there
are two lights in our living room. We have
got a very big TV. There is a CD player on
our bookshelf. I think our living room is nice.

Grammar

there is – there are

How to say what is or is not there:

In Rick's bedroom **there is** a big desk and **there are** two windows.
In Tina's bedroom **there isn't** a desk.
There aren't many books on her shelf.

Present progressive

How to say what someone is doing now or what is happening now:

FORMATION: Person + am / is / are + ing-form of the verb

Can you help me? – Sorry, **I'm doing** my homework.
Where's Joan? – **She's having** a shower.
Where are the boys? – **They're playing** football.
Help me, mum. – Sorry, **I'm cooking**.
Where's Sandra? – **She's watching TV**.
Where's Alan? – **He's watching TV**.
Boys, where are you? – **We're cleaning** our bikes.

Yes, I'm learning grammar.
COMICS

UNIT 14

Happy Birthday

1 Picture dictionary

The months of the year

January
February
March
April
May
June
July
August
September
October
November
December

2

Practise the ordinal numbers. Then ask your classmates.

1st	the first	11th	the eleventh	21st	the twenty-first
2nd	the second	12th	the twelfth	22nd	the twenty-second
3rd	the third	13th	the thirteenth	30th	the thirtieth
4th	the fourth	14th	the fourteenth	40th	the fortieth
5th	the fifth	15th	the fifteenth	50th	the fiftieth
6th	the sixth	16th	the sixteenth	60th	the sixtieth
7th	the seventh	17th	the seventeenth	70th	the seventieth
8th	the eighth	18th	the eighteenth	80th	the eightieth
9th	the ninth	19th	the nineteenth	90th	the ninetieth
10th	the tenth	20th	the twentieth	100th	the hundredth

When's your birthday?

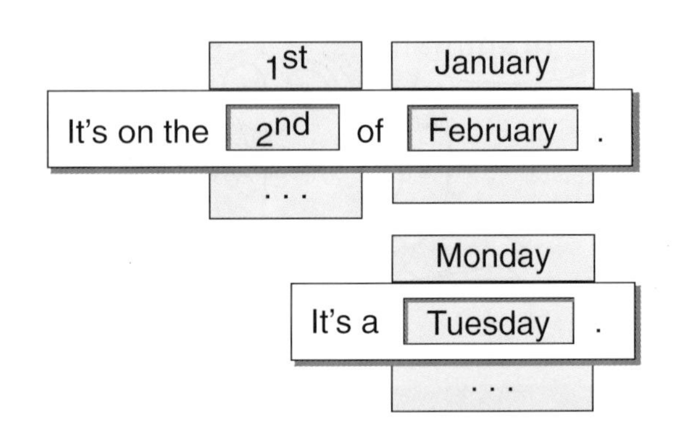

What day is it this year?

3 A story

Read the text.

Maggie's birthday present

February 14th is a wonderful day for Maggie. It is her birthday. She is eleven years old. In the morning she opens her birthday cards. She is very happy. She has twelve cards from her friends and three from her family.
Maggie gets home from school at five o'clock. Then she has a small party with her mother, her two brothers and three schoolfriends. There is a big birthday cake with eleven candles on it. Maggie, her brothers and her friends eat lots of the cake. "Open your presents now!" her brothers say. "Yes, open your presents!" say her friends. There is a book, a nice biro and a music cassette from her friends.
Then she opens the present from her brother Michael. It is a red plastic bowl. She looks at it and thinks: "What a funny present!" and says: "Thank you very much, Mike." Then she opens the present from her brother Richard. It is a small rubber ball. She looks at it and thinks: "A rubber ball? For me? A very funny present." "Thank you very much, Rick," she says. "And here's my present for you," says her mother. Maggie opens it and finds a big brown brush. "A plastic bowl, a rubber ball, and now a big brush! How funny!" Maggie thinks.
"Do you like it?" says her mother, and smiles. "Erm . . . yes. Thank you," Maggie says. "No, I don't," she thinks. Her brothers and her mother laugh. "Do you really like your presents?" Mike says. Maggie does not know what to say. Her mother says, "Come with me." They all go out into the garden. And there in a basket is the present for Maggie: a beautiful little dog. Maggie takes the dog out of the basket, kisses it and laughs. "So the bowl and the brush and the ball are all for you!"

4

Write the correct numbers in the small boxes.
Then write the sentences in your exercise book.

① February the fourteenth is	☐ friends eat lots of the cake.
② Maggie gets home from school	☐ a plastic bowl and a rubber ball.
③ Maggie, her brothers and her	☐ there is a wonderful present for Maggie.
④ Then Maggie opens	☐ Maggie's birthday.
⑤ Maggie's brothers give her	☐ at five o'clock, and then she has a small party.
⑥ Maggie gets a	☐ her presents.
⑦ Maggie does not	☐ brush from her mother.
⑧ But in the garden	☐ like her presents.

5

Now listen to the cassette. Then work in groups.
Act out what happens at Maggie's birthday party.
There are four roles: Maggie, her mother and her brothers, Michael and Richard.

When's your birthday?
On the eighth of June.

6 A song

Listen to the cassette
and do the birthday-song game.

Pronunciation

Listen and find out which parts of the following words are stressed.
Examples:

angry	■ □	
around		□ ■

poster			window		
second			nothing		
below			about		
toothbrush			away		
behind			cupboard		

Study and change

Text 1

My birthday is on June 8th.
It is a Tuesday this year.
Then I can give a little party
for my friends and my two sisters.
I want to have a big birthday cake
with eleven candles.
For my birthday present I want
a mountain bike or a new cassette recorder.
I love birthdays.

I love birthdays.

Text 2

I have got a friend.
He is in my class at school.
His name is Kevin. Kevin is twelve.
His birthday is on September 20th.
It is a Thursday this year. I like Kevin's parties.
They are great fun.
We sit at a table in the garden
and eat hamburgers and lots
and lots of chips with ketchup.
We drink coke and orange juice.
Then we sing songs and dance.
Then we give Kevin his presents.

NOTE
You write:
My birthday is on June 8th.
You say:
My birthday's on the eighth of June.
Or:
My birthday's on June the eighth.

Grammar

	Cardinal numbers	Ordinal numbers
1	one	the first
2	two	the second
17	seventeen	the seventeenth
58	fifty-eight	the fifty-eighth
100	a hundred	the hundredth

UNIT 15

Breakfast

1 Picture dictionary

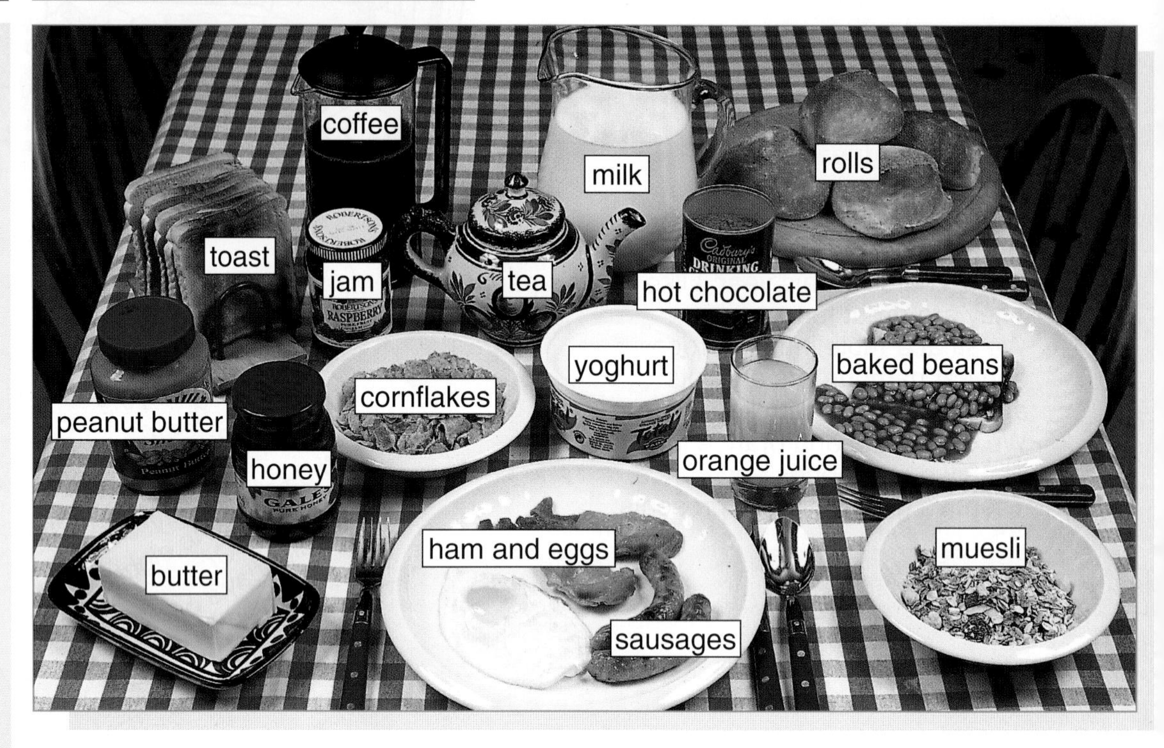

2

Listen to the cassette.
Tick ✔ the breakfast words you hear.

☐ baked beans	☐ jam	☐ sausages
☐ coffee	☐ milk	☐ tea
☐ cornflakes	☐ muesli	☐ toast
☐ ham and eggs	☐ orange juice	☐ yoghurt
☐ honey	☐ peanut butter	☐ butter
☐ hot chocolate	☐ rolls	☐ apple juice

3

Listen to the cassette.
Read the dialogue. Then act it out in pairs.

Carol and Steven at the breakfast table

Steven: What's for breakfast?
Carol: Muesli, yoghurt and toast.
Steven: Yuk! No, thank you!
Carol: Well, what would you like then?
Steven: I'd like some ham and eggs or some sausages and eggs.
Carol: Sorry, we don't eat ham or sausages or eggs.
Steven: No?
I eat them every day.
Well, have you got baked beans then?
Carol: Yes, I think so.
Steven: OK, I'd like some baked beans on toast, please.
Carol: Baked beans on toast for breakfast?
Steven: Yeah, it's great.
Can I make some?
Carol: Yes, OK.
Steven: Would you like some too?
Carol: No, I . . . Erm . . . Oh yes, please!

4 Grammar rhythm

Listen to the first part. Fill in the blanks with **a**, **an** *or* **some**.
Then listen to the second part and say it yourself.

______ milk
______ honey
______ apple
______ apples
______ roll

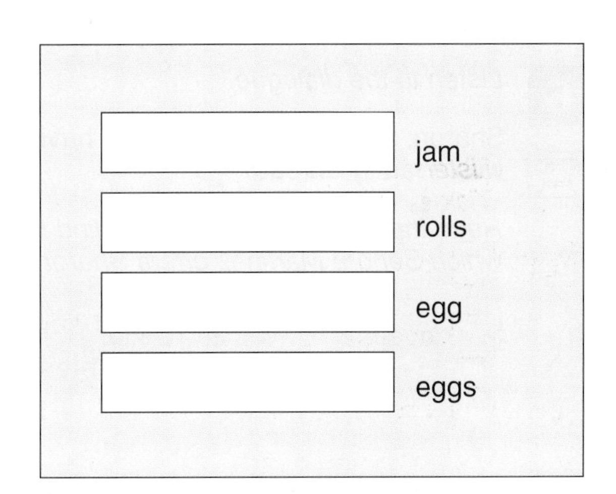

______ jam
______ rolls
______ egg
______ eggs

I' d like some rolls.

I' d like an egg.

5 Grammar rhythm

Work with a partner. Guess what the man and the woman are saying. Fill in the missing letters. Then listen to the cassette.

The American breakfast

I'd like some m _ _ _ ,
some j _ _ _ _ , s _ _ _ t _ _ _ _ ,
s _ _ _ c _ _ _ _ _ _ , a _ e _ _ ,
a b _ _ _ _ _ a _ _ s _ _ _ h _ _ .

I'm sorry, terribly sorry.
The fridge is empty.

Huh? Well, what about
s _ _ _ _ _ _ g?

Great idea, honey,
b _ _ w _ h _ _ _ _ 't got t _ _ m _ _ _ _ .

6

Listen to the dialogue.

Sharon, an English schoolgirl, is having her first breakfast with a family abroad.

Read through this list and underline the things which Señora Martinez offers Sharon:

an apple   rolls and butter   ham and eggs   jam   a banana   sausages
toast   muesli   bread and cheese   yoghurt   cornflakes

7

Listen to the cassette again. Read through this list and underline the things which Sharon chooses:

sausages   toast   muesli   cornflakes   ham and eggs   yoghurt
milk   rolls and butter

8 The monster breakfast game

Work in groups.

A friendly monster comes to your house.
He is very hungry. But he does not like
what you like for breakfast.
Your teacher tells each group
what their monster likes.

Write down what you can give him to eat.

9

Listen to the other groups. They read out their lists.
Then say:

We think their monster eats things with ... / ... / ... in them.

10

Look at the words in the box. Ask your teacher:

What does "plate" / "ring" / "..." mean?

ring
answer the telephone
jump onto
plate
more
drop

11 A story

The cat's favourite breakfast

Look at the pictures. Then read through the texts below. Match the texts to the pictures. Write the correct number in each box.

☐ Mr Parker comes back into the kitchen. He looks at his plate. "Where are my sausages?" he says.

☐ Suddenly the telephone rings. So he goes out of the kitchen to answer it.

☐ His cat wants some breakfast too. "Not now, I'm eating!" says Mr Parker.

☐ Mr Parker sees the mouse on his plate. "Oh, my goodness!" he says and drops the sausages on the floor.

☐ The cat jumps onto the table and eats the sausages.

☐ One morning Mr Parker is in the kitchen. He is eating sausages and baked beans for breakfast.

☐ Behind his back the cat puts a mouse on his plate.

☐ So he cooks some more sausages.

Study and change

Text 1

I have toast and
peanut butter for breakfast,
and I drink two cups of tea.
My mother and sister have
muesli and yoghurt.
My mother has coffee and
my sister has tea.

Text 2*

I have an egg and some toast for breakfast,
but on Sundays I like to have cornflakes
or muesli. I drink a glass of milk or
some fruit juice. My mother and father have
a roll and a cup of coffee, but on Sundays
they have ham and eggs and toast
and coffee.

Grammar

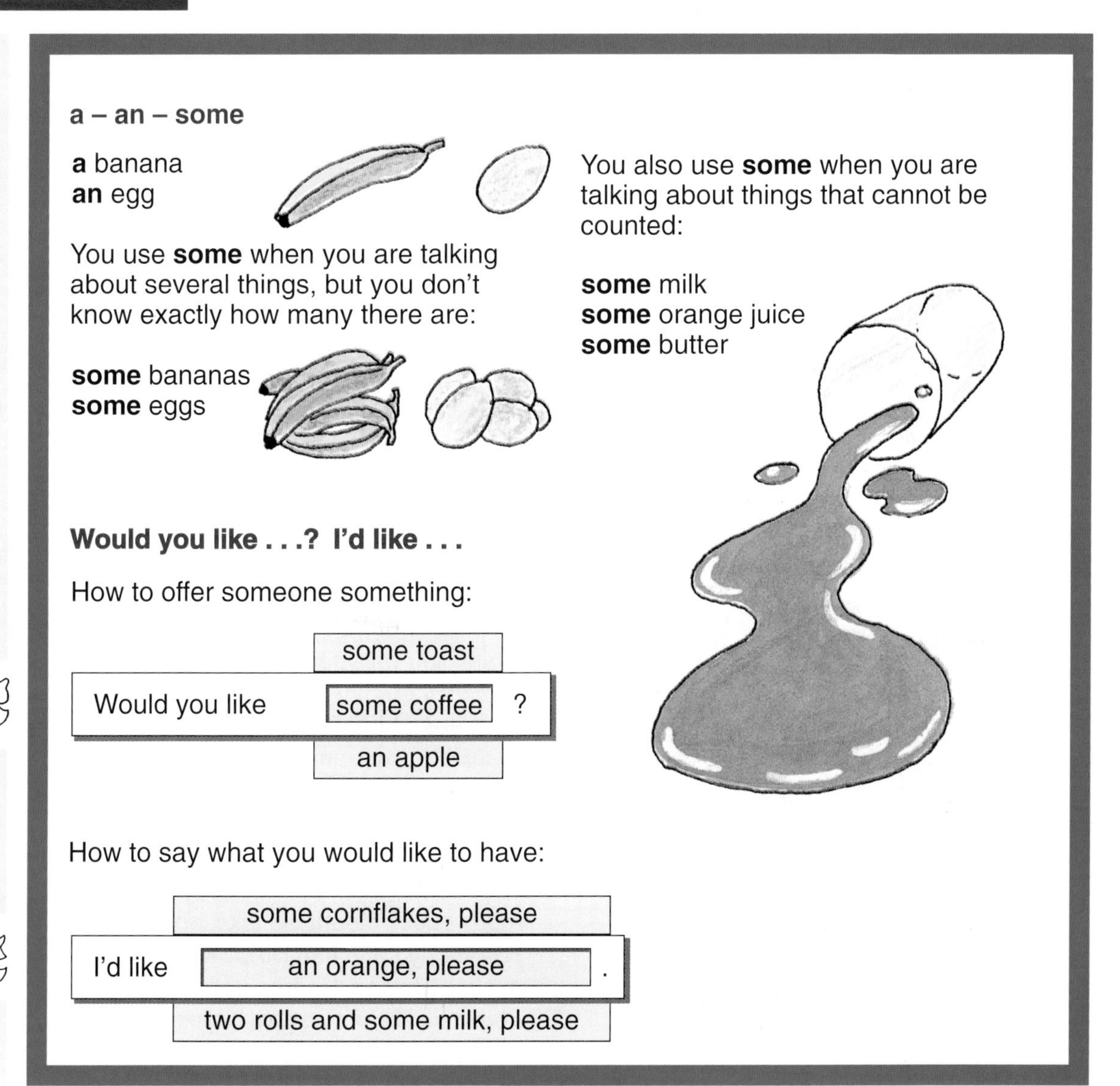

a – an – some

a banana
an egg

You use **some** when you are talking about several things, but you don't know exactly how many there are:

some bananas
some eggs

You also use **some** when you are talking about things that cannot be counted:

some milk
some orange juice
some butter

Would you like . . .? I'd like . . .

How to offer someone something:

Would you like some toast / some coffee / an apple ?

How to say what you would like to have:

I'd like some cornflakes, please / an orange, please / two rolls and some milk, please .

UNIT 16

Brothers, sisters and friends

1 *Work with a partner.*
Find the poem by filling in the words from the boxes.
Then listen to the cassette and check.

My brother and sister

My sister's name is ______________________.
My brother's name is ______________________.
My sister is really ______________________.
My brother is really ______________________.

great
Kate
bad
Brad

My sister says, ______________________.
My brother says, ______________________.
My sister likes to ______________________.
My brother likes to ______________________.

shout
"Come in"
"Get out"
sing

My sister wants to ______________________.
My brother wants to ______________________.
My sister is a ______________________.
My brother is a ______________________.

rest
sweetie
pest
play with me

NOTE
She is nice.
She is **really** nice!

2 *Look at the picture.*
Then read through the letter.

Dear Lisa,
Thank you for your letter and the photos. I like them a lot.
Here is a photo of me and my friends Adrian and Roy. They go to my school. We really like our class, but our teacher gives us a lot of homework.
Adrian is great fun. He has got a really super mountain bike, so everybody calls him Biker. Roy is my best friend. He has got two dogs. We like playing with them.
Keith

3 *Now talk about Keith and his friends.*
Start like this:

Keith has got two friends. They go . . .
They like . . .
His friend Adrian . . .
His friend Roy . . .

4 *Read the sentences below. Then listen to the interviews with Sylvia, Tom and Jane.*
Tick ✔ the true sentences. Then correct the other sentences.

- ☐ Sylvia has got a sister.
- ☐ Her sister is twelve.
- ☐ Her name is Ronny.
- ☐ Sylvia likes her sister a lot.
- ☐ Her sister helps her with her homework.

- ☐ Tom has got a brother.
- ☐ Tom has got a lot of friends.
- ☐ His best friend's name is John Mortimer.
- ☐ John is a boy from Tom's class.
- ☐ Tom plays tennis with John.

Sylvia Tom Jane

- ☐ Jane has got two brothers and two sisters.
- ☐ Her two brothers are seventeen and fifteen.
- ☐ Her brother Johnny loves sweets.
- ☐ Everybody calls him "Honey".
- ☐ Jane likes her sisters, Sarah and Isabel.

5 *Study the language below.*
Then talk about yourself and your sister(s), brother(s) or friend(s).

Brother(s), sister(s)

I have got [. . .] brother(s) and [. . .] sister(s).

My [brother's / sister's] name is [. . .] .

My [brothers' / sisters'] names are [. . .] and [. . .] .

My [brother / sister] [. . .] is [. . .] (years old).

NOTE
My brother**'s** name is Jack.
My brother**s'** names are Tom and Dick.

Friends

I haven't got a brother or a sister, but I have got lots of friends.

My	best friend's name is	...	.
	best friends' names are	... and ...	

I	play football	with	him	.
	play volleyball		her	
	listen to cassettes		them	
	watch videos			
	...			

6 A story

Read the following text. Then do the exercise on the following page.

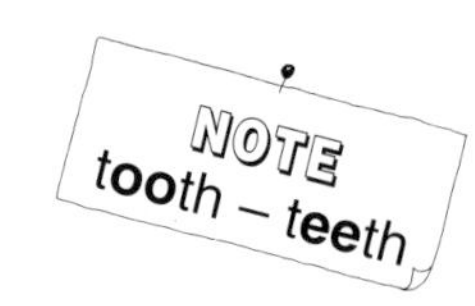

Christopher

Christopher is eight. He has blue eyes and brown hair. When he smiles, you can see that one of his front teeth is missing. Then he looks really funny. Everybody likes Christopher. "He's a nice boy," says Mr Stevens, the postman. "He looks so sweet," says Mrs Mitchell, his teacher. "He's my darling," says his mother.
But there is one problem with Christopher. He is my brother. And I don't think he is a nice boy. I don't think he looks sweet. And he is not my darling. I think Christopher is a real pest.
When I want to watch television, he wants to play music.
When I want to play music, he wants to sleep.
And when I want to sleep, he wants to sing songs.
Christopher is a real pest.
I have also got a friend.
Her name is Trish. Trish has not got a brother or a sister.
When she wants to watch television, nobody wants to play music.
When she wants to play music, nobody wants to sleep.
And when she wants to sleep, nobody wants to sing songs.
I think that's really great. Trish says it's boring.
She says that she doesn't want to be alone.
She says that she wants a brother.
Maybe she is right.
Maybe it is good to have a brother. Maybe Christopher isn't such a pest. Maybe, just maybe, mum is right.

Complete the sentences:

You can see that one of his front teeth is missing.
Mr Stevens thinks Christopher is a nice boy.
Mrs Mitchell says that Christopher looks so sweet.
Christopher is his mother's darling.
When Christopher's sister wants to watch television, he wants to play music.
Christopher's sister thinks he is a real pest.
Trish has not got a brother.
When she wants to watch television, nobody wants to play music.
"Maybe it is good to have a brother," Christopher's sister thinks.

7 A song

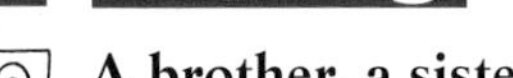

A brother, a sister, a friend

When I watch TV,
he wants to play with me.
When I want to play,
he wants to sleep.
When I want to sleep,
he wants to sing a song.
Isn't my brother a pest?

When I want to play,
she wants to watch TV.
When I want to sleep,
she wants to play.
When I want to sing a song,
she wants to sleep.
Isn't my sister a pest?

But maybe it's good to have a sister.
Maybe, just maybe, mum knows best.
Maybe it's good to have a brother.
A brother or a sister is not a pest.

Oh yes, it's good to have a brother,
oh yes, it's good to have a friend,
oh yes, it's good to have a sister.
And now this song comes to an end.

8

Talk about problems you have with a brother or a sister or a friend.

When I want to	watch TV / read a book / sleep / **play music** / play computer games / play football / do my homework	,	**he** / she	wants to	. . .	.

9 Look at the cartoon.
Work with a partner and put the speech bubbles below into the correct order by filling in numbers from 1 to 12.
Then listen to the cassette and check.
Finally, act out the dialogue.

(6) Good night, little one.
I'm really sorry for you.

(3) No, Mike. It's time for bed.

(4) But mum! Susan is still up.

(1) Mike, it's eight o'clock.
Time for you to go to bed.

(10) Sorry, Susan, there are no more chocolate bananas.

(2) But mum! I want to see the show.

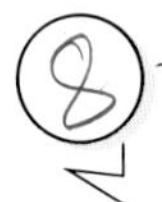
(7) OK. Mum, can I have a chocolate banana before I go?

(8) OK, here you are.
But don't forget to brush your teeth.

(5) Susan is thirteen, and you're ten.

(9) Can I have one too, mum?

(12) Good night, big one.
I'm really sorry for you.

(11) But mum! I want one too.

10 Creative grammar practice

Read the two texts. Study them, then cover them up. Try to reconstruct the texts with the help of the language below. Then write your own text about your sister, brother or friend.

My brother
He likes football,
he likes his friend Caroline,
he likes his bike,
but
there's one thing
he
doesn't like:
computer games.

My sister
She likes music,
she likes pets,
she likes good stories,
but
there are two things
she
doesn't like:
unfair friends and chocolate pudding.

My sister/brother/friend

she likes Chocdate,
she likes Ice cream,
she likes drama,
but
there are two things she
doesn't like: Jelly and pudding.

Study and change

Text 1

I have got a brother.
His name is Peter and he is fourteen. We call him "Pete". Pete is very nice and he plays with me a lot. But when he feels bad, he goes to his room. Then he doesn't come out for a long time.

Text 2*

I have got two sisters. Their names are Sandra and Cathie. Sandra is eight and Cathie is sixteen. Sandra and I think Cathie is great. She often plays games with us. There is one problem with Cathie. When her boyfriend Nick is with her, she doesn't want to see or hear us. Then we don't like her.

Grammar

Some words that stand in for nouns

Examples:

Listen to **Bob.** → Listen to **him.**
Look at **Mary.** → Look at **her.**
Please, help **me and my sister.** → Please, help **us.**
I can't find my **jeans.** → I can't find **them.**

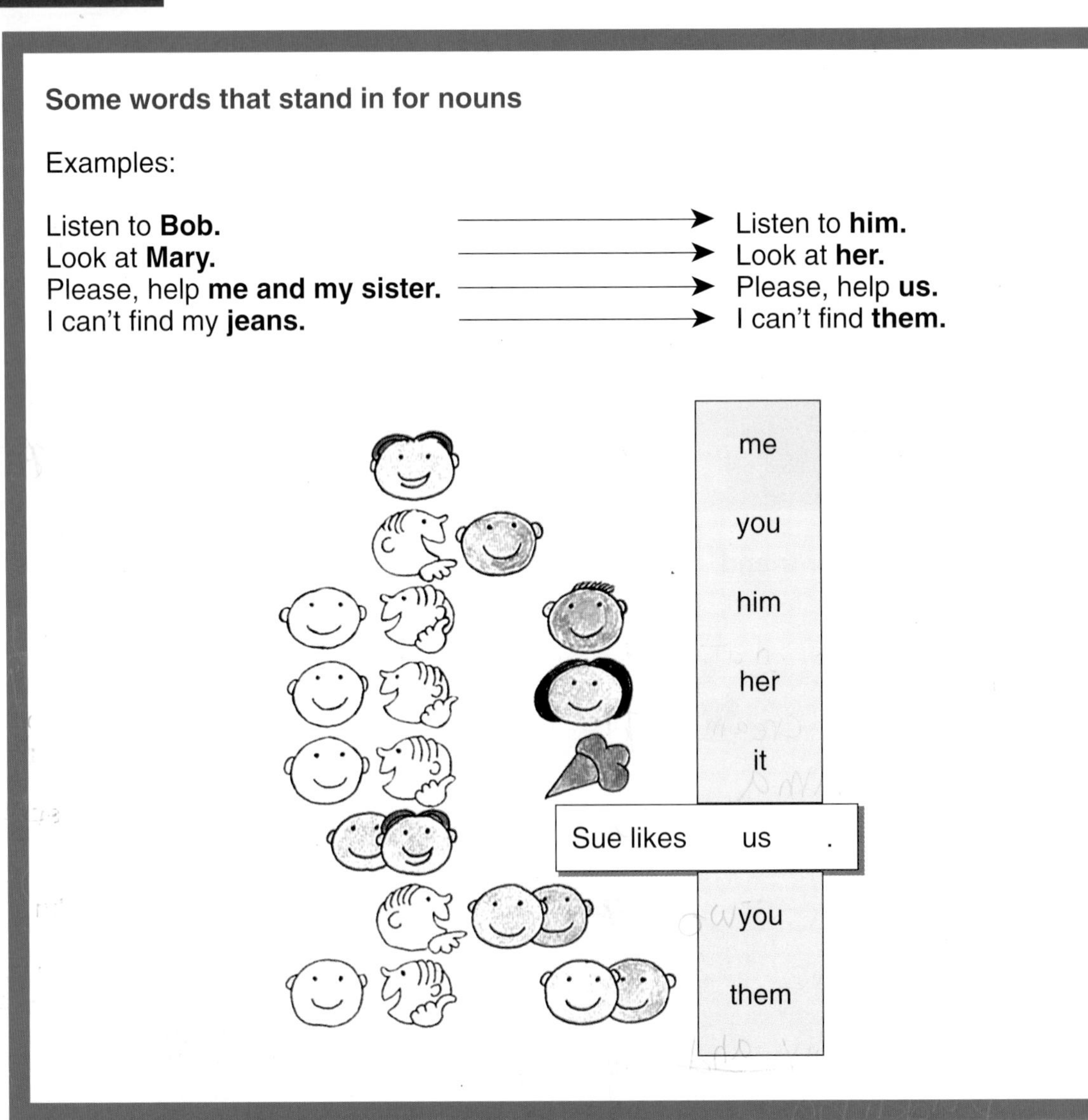

UNIT 17

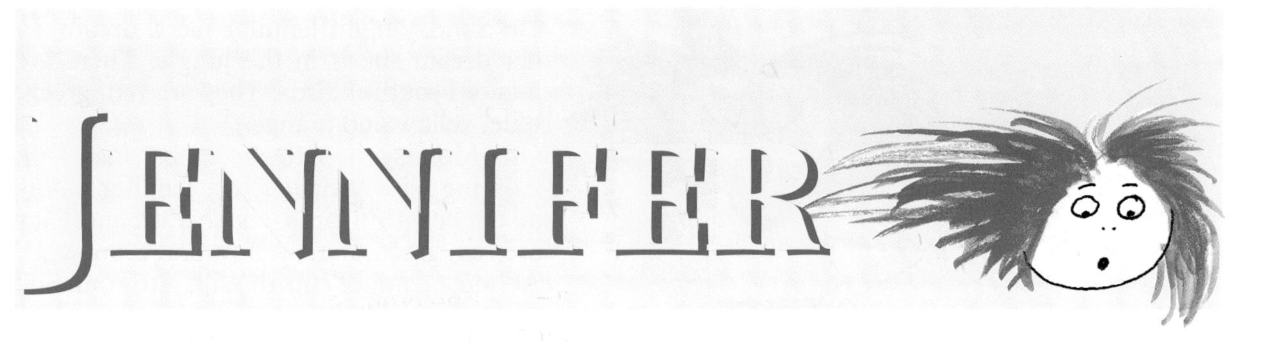

1 Picture dictionary

2 A story

Read the story.

Jennifer's new jeans

"Mum, can I have a new pair of jeans?" Jennifer asks. "New jeans?" her mum says. "Why?"

"Because my jeans are full of stains. There are glue stains, ink stains, grass stains and oil stains from my bike."

"I'm sorry, dear. But I can't buy you new jeans right now. Sorry."

Jennifer goes back to her room. She feels very unhappy. She looks at her old jeans. "There are a lot of stains on them," she thinks.

"I want new jeans."

On Sunday night Jennifer has a dream. In her dream she is in the jungle. There are lots of beautiful birds. They are red, green, blue, yellow and orange.

On Monday Jennifer's class does silk painting with their teacher. Jennifer paints all the beautiful birds from her dream. They are red, green, blue, yellow and orange.

At home Jennifer cuts the silk birds out. She sews them on the jeans where the stains are. Jennifer looks at her jeans. "They look great," she thinks.

The next day Jennifer puts on her jeans with the birds. Her friends look at her jeans. "Your jeans look super," they say. Jennifer is very happy.

A few days later all the boys and girls in Jennifer's class have got beautiful silk birds on their jeans. They are red, green, blue, yellow and orange.

"What a jungle," Mrs Quentin, their teacher, says and smiles.

3

Put the sentences into the correct order.
Write the numbers (1 to 10) in the circles.

She sews the silk birds on her jeans where the stains are.

Jennifer's friends like her jeans very much.

Jennifer paints the birds from her dream.

Jennifer asks her mother for a new pair of jeans.

On Monday Jennifer's class does silk painting with their teacher.

On Sunday night she has a dream.

Her mother says she cannot buy her new jeans.

At home she cuts the silk birds out.

In her dream she sees lots of beautiful birds.

Jennifer is very unhappy.

4

Now close your books.
Listen to the story on cassette.
Then work with a partner.
Write down all the words
you can remember from the story.
How many words can you remember?

5

Listen to four interviews with children. Tick ✔ the correct answers.

Patricia

- [ ] likes
- [ ] does not like

the story.

Because

- [ ] there is a happy ending.
- [ ] Jennifer is a clever girl.
- [ ] she thinks birds on jeans are ugly.
- [ ] she thinks the ending is not good.

Simon

- [ ] likes
- [ ] does not like

the story.

Because

- [ ] there is a happy ending.
- [ ] Jennifer is a clever girl.
- [ ] he thinks birds on jeans are ugly.
- [ ] he thinks the ending is not good.

Keith

- [ ] likes
- [ ] does not like

the story.

Because

- [ ] there is a happy ending.
- [ ] he thinks Jennifer has a good idea.
- [ ] he thinks birds on jeans are ugly.
- [ ] he doesn't like the ending.

Cindy

- [ ] likes
- [ ] does not like

the story.

Because

- [ ] Jennifer's friends think her jeans are great.
- [ ] she thinks Jennifer has a good idea.
- [ ] she thinks birds on jeans are ugly.
- [ ] she doesn't like the ending.

6 Picture dictionary

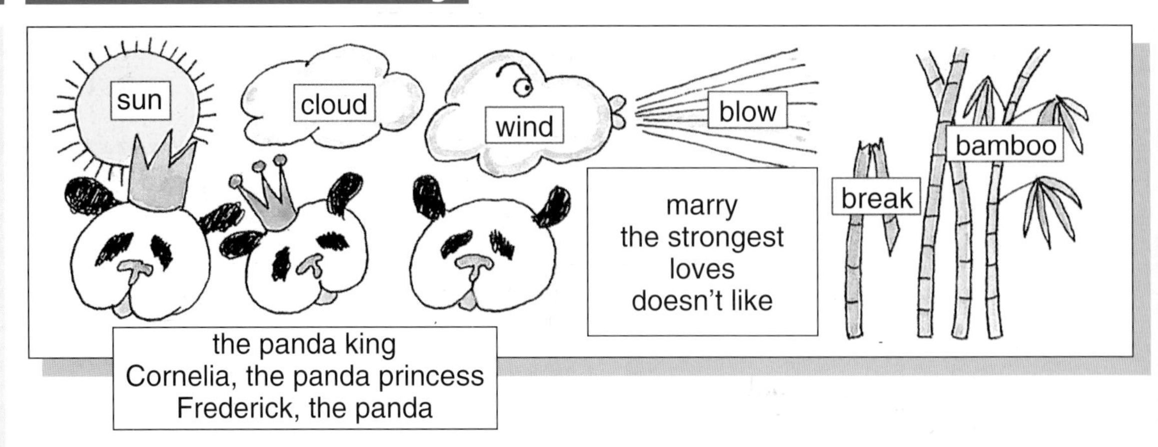

7

The words in the picture dictionary are from Jennifer's favourite story "The panda princess".

Look at the words. What is the story about?

I think the story is about . . . .

I think there is / are . . . .

I think the panda king / the Panda Princess / Frederick, the panda / the wind / the sun likes / doesn't like / loves / breaks / blows / is . . . .

8

Listen to Jennifer's favourite story "The panda princess". Then mark the following sentences true (T) or false (F).

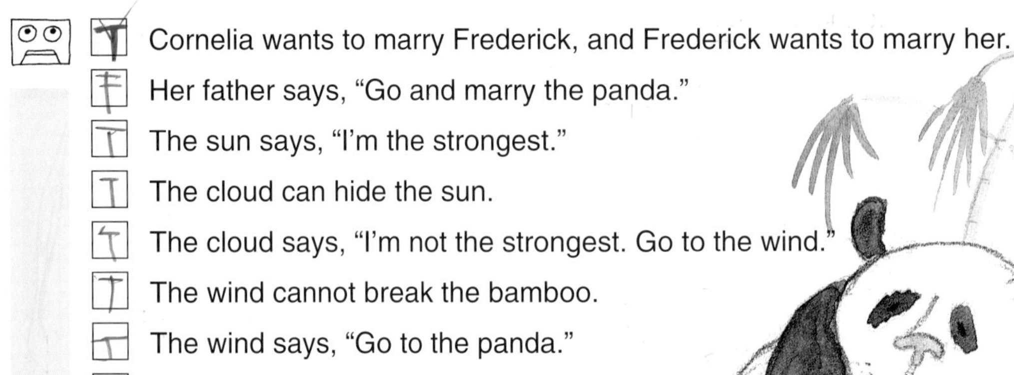

- Cornelia wants to marry Frederick, and Frederick wants to marry her.
- Her father says, "Go and marry the panda."
- The sun says, "I'm the strongest."
- The cloud can hide the sun.
- The cloud says, "I'm not the strongest. Go to the wind."
- The wind cannot break the bamboo.
- The wind says, "Go to the panda."
- The bamboo says, "I'm the strongest."
- Cornelia is happy because the bamboo says, "Frederick is the strongest."

9 *Who says what in the story? Mark the speech bubbles.*

princess: p
king: k
wind: w
sun: s
cloud: c
bamboo: b

You cannot marry a panda, Cornelia. K

Why not? I love Frederick. I want to marry him, and he wants to marry me. p

k No, no, no, no. You're a panda princess and a panda princess cannot marry a panda. You must marry the sun.

The sun? Why the sun? B

b Because the sun is the strongest.

S I'm not the strongest. Go to the cloud.

The cloud? Why? P

S Because the cloud can hide me. The cloud is the strongest.

C I'm not the strongest. Go to the wind.

The wind? Why? P

Because the wind can blow me away. The wind is the strongest. C

W I'm not the strongest. Go to the bamboo.

The bamboo? Why? P

W Because I cannot break the bamboo. The bamboo is the strongest.

b I'm not the strongest. Go to Frederick, the panda.

Frederick? Why Frederick? P

b Because he is the strongest.

Frederick is the strongest? Why is he the strongest? P

b Because he can eat me.

10

Now listen to the cassette again.
Then work in groups of six. Act out the story.
There are six roles: the panda king, Cornelia, the sun, the cloud, the wind and the bamboo.

11 A song

Don't ask me why

Why?
Don't ask me why.
Why?
Don't ask me why.

Why do we come to class through the door?
Because we can't come to class through the floor.
Why is coffee brown and not blue?
Because I am me and you are you.

Why?
Don't ask me why.
Why?
Don't ask me why.

Why does the day come after the night?
Because the other way round just isn't right.
Why do you go to school?
Because I don't want to be a fool.

Why?
Don't ask me why.
Why?
Don't ask me why.

Why haven't we got four or five legs?
Why don't we eat ice cream on eggs?
Because a hamburger isn't a snake,
and because we don't put ketchup on cake.

Why?
Don't ask me why.
Why?
Don't ask me why.

Why can't I ask you why?
Because I'll start to cry.

Why?

Pronunciation

Listen to the words on the cassette and ✔ tick the sound you hear.

	[s]	[z]
bananas	☐	☐
bikes	☐	☐
chips	☐	☐
badges	☐	☐
beans	☐	☐
stamps	☐	☐

	[s]	[z]
hands	☐	☐
coins	☐	☐
coats	☐	☐
noises	☐	☐
stars	☐	☐
bags	☐	☐

Text writing

Look at the pictures and write what happens.

Flowers

HAPPY BIRTHDAY!

Grammar

why – because

How to ask the reason for something:

How to give a reason:

Why are you so unhappy?
Because my jeans are full of stains.

UNIT 18

What's on TV?

1 *Look at the television sets.*
Write in the names of the programmes.

the news
cartoon
nature programme
sports programme
quiz
western
romantic film
detective film

2 *Listen to the cassette. Look at the TV sets in* **1** *and fill in the numbers.*
Then talk with a partner.

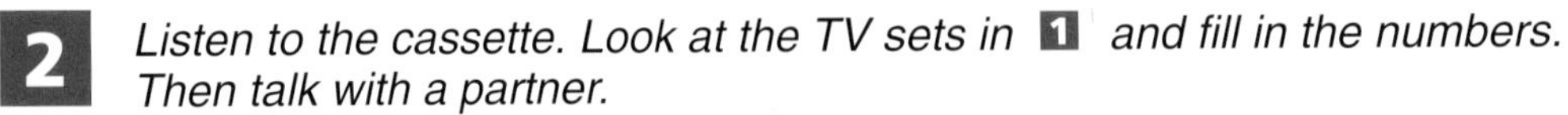

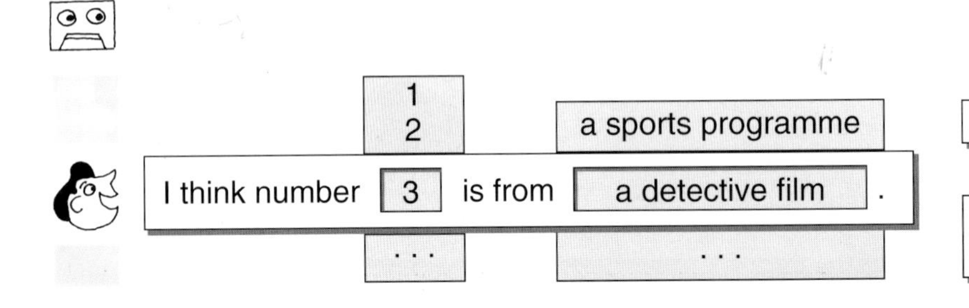

1
2
I think number 3 is from a sports programme
a detective film
. . .
. . .

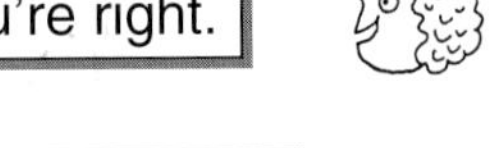

I think you're right.

No, I don't think so.
I think it's from a . . .

3 *Make sentences about yourself.*

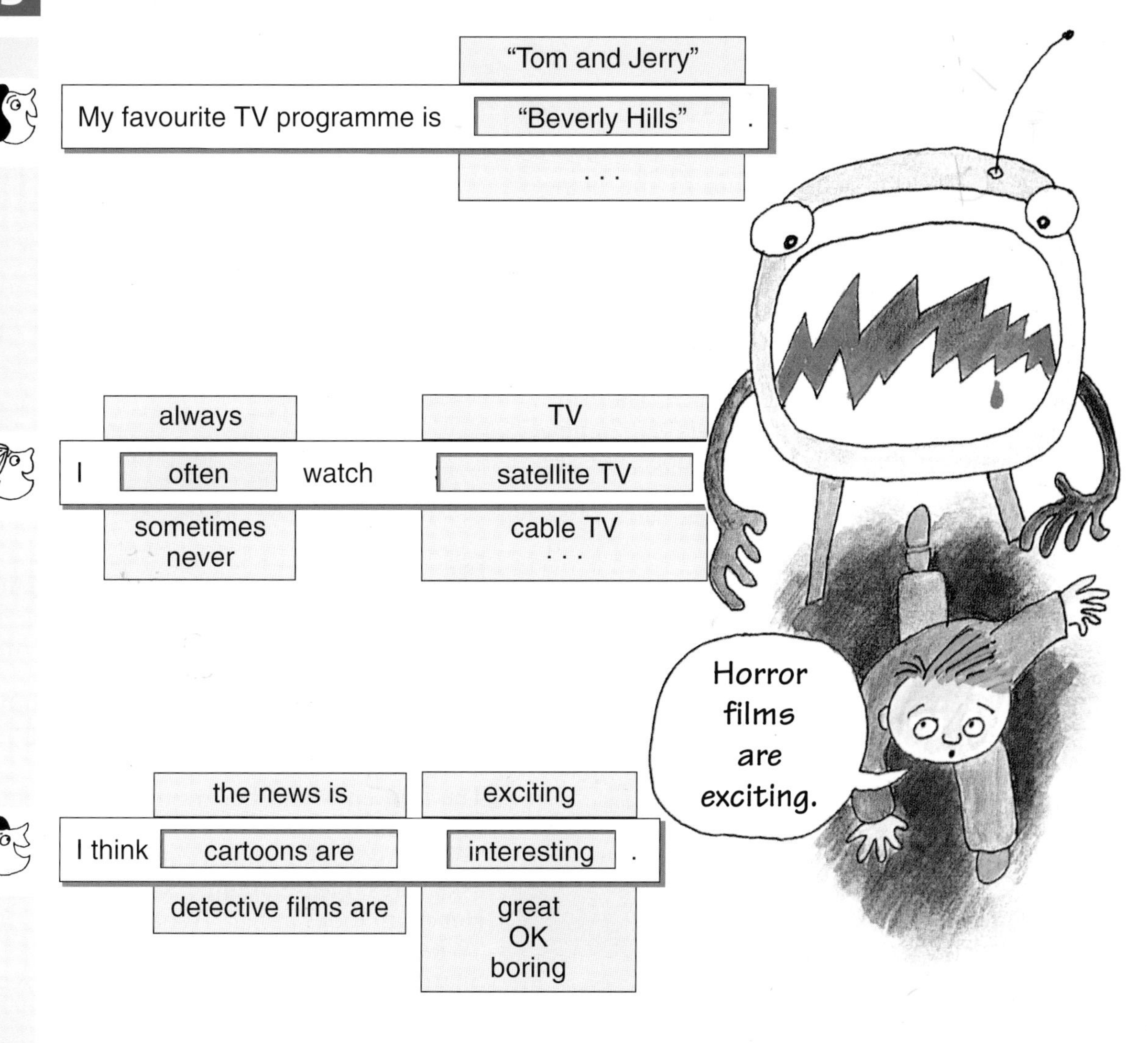

"Tom and Jerry"
My favourite TV programme is "Beverly Hills" .
. . .
always
I often watch
sometimes
never
TV
satellite TV
cable TV
. . .
the news is
I think cartoons are
detective films are
exciting
interesting .
great
OK
boring
Horror films are exciting.

4 Picture dictionary

5 A story

Read this story.

The golden bracelet

Sharon is sitting on the sofa in the living room. She is watching her favourite TV programme "Kim's Island". Sharon always watches it.
Kim is a young Indian boy.
He lives on a tropical island.
This week Kim is in the jungle. He goes into a cave. He finds a box. He opens it. There are two golden bracelets in it. Kim is very happy. He looks at the bracelets and does not see the snake.
"Kim! Kim!" Sharon shouts.
"What is it?" Kim answers.
"A snake," Sharon shouts.
"Where?"
"Behind you," Sharon answers. "There!"
Kim turns round. He sees the snake and stands very still. He looks at the snake.
The snake looks at him.
Then the snake goes away.

"Thank you, Sharon," Kim says. "Thank you very much." He smiles at her. "This is for you." And he gives Sharon one of the two golden bracelets.
"Oh, thank you!" she says. "It's beautiful!"
"I'm dreaming," Sharon thinks. "This is a dream."
The film ends and her mother comes into the room.
"Would you like some orange juice?" she asks. "Yes, please, mum," Sharon answers.
Her mum looks at her. "What's this?"
"What?"
Sharon turns round. On the sofa she sees the beautiful golden bracelet!

6

True or false?

- [ ] Sharon is sitting on the sofa in her room.
- [ ] Sharon's favourite TV programme is "Kim's Island".
- [ ] In a cave in the jungle Kim finds a box.
- [ ] There is a snake in the box.
- [ ] Sharon sees the snake and shouts: "Kim! Kim!"
- [ ] Kim sees the snake and runs away.
- [ ] Kim gives Sharon the two golden bracelets.
- [ ] Sharon thinks this is a dream.
- [ ] Her mum comes in and gives her a cup of tea.
- [ ] The golden bracelet is on the sofa in the living room.

7 *Listen to the story "The golden bracelet" on cassette.*
Then work in groups of four. Act out the story.
There are four roles: Kim, Sharon, the snake and mum.

Pronunciation

Listen to the words on the cassette and repeat them.
Then listen again and ✔ tick the sound you hear.

	[tʃ]	[dʒ]
generous	☐	☐
jacket	☐	☐
chicken	☐	☐
jeans	☐	☐
badge	☐	☐

	[tʃ]	[dʒ]
kitchen	☐	☐
catch	☐	☐
just	☐	☐
chocolate	☐	☐
juice	☐	☐

Study and change

Text 1

I like watching TV.
My favourite programmes are sports and detective films.
I always watch TV on Saturday and Sunday in the afternoon and in the evening.
I also like cartoons.
I hate romantic films and the news. My father thinks the news is interesting.

Text 2 ★

I like watching TV in the evening, but I don't like watching it in the morning or the afternoon. There are many interesting films. I often watch nature programmes. I think they are very interesting.
I like seeing animals from other countries.
My brother often watches westerns, but I don't like them. I think they are boring.
My sister likes quizzes.

Grammar

always – often – sometimes – never

How to say how often someone does something:

I **always** have muesli for breakfast.
He has **often** got a cold.
They **sometimes** watch romantic films.
She **sometimes** wears skirts to school.
I **never** watch "Tom and Jerry".
We **never** swap things.

UNIT 19

The box of nuts

1 Picture dictionary

2

Look at the words in the picture dictionary and try to make up a story. Use as many words from the picture dictionary as you like. Start like this:

I think the story is about . . .
First the . . .
Then the . . .

3 A story

Read the story.

The box of nuts

Crickwood is a small place in the west of England.
There are a lot of small farms and big woods.
In the woods and fields there are a lot of animals:
birds, foxes, rabbits and . . . Mick, Pam and Dave, three hamsters.
On a nice summer day they are sitting under a big tree
near Joe Binham's farm.

Mick: There are some wonderful nuts in a box on the kitchen table. Joe's wife wants to bake a cake with them.
Dave: Really? I love nuts.
Pam: Me too. Can't we get them?
Dave: No, I don't think so. Think of the dog.
Mick: The Binhams are all working in the fields. The dog is with them.
Pam: But the problem is: how can we get into the kitchen?
Mick: I don't know.
Dave: Let me think . . . Joe always puts the key under the doormat. Listen. We can put the key into the lock and if we all hang on to it, we can open the door.
Pam: Great. Let's go.
Mick: Okay.

So the three clever hamsters steal the nuts. They want to eat them
under the big tree near the pond. They have got the big box full of nuts
and it is very heavy. Dave is very tired and in the wood he falls down.
Some of the nuts fall into the grass.
Near the big tree he falls down again. More nuts fall into the grass.

Dave: Let's eat the nuts now. I'm hungry.
Mick: Good idea.
Pam: The nuts in the box are for Mick and me. Your nuts are in the grass.
Mick: Go and look for them, Dave.

So Mick and Pam send Dave away. Dave is sad.
He runs into the wood. Mick and Pam are happy.
They swim in the pond and
then they eat all the nuts.

THE END

4

True or false?

- In the woods and fields near Crickwood there are lots of animals.
- Joe Binham has got three hamsters: Mick, Pam and Dave.
- The hamsters are sitting in a tree and eating nuts.
- The key to the kitchen is under the doormat.
- Mick and Pam open the door for Dave.
- The dog is sitting in the kitchen.
- Dave is very tired and he falls down.
- Dave, Mick and Pam swim in the pond. Then they eat all the nuts.

5

Do you like the ending of the story "The box of nuts"?
No? Okay, here is another ending.

Ending number 2:

When Mick and Pam want to go back to their tree, they see Joe's dog in front of them. He takes Mick and Pam in his mouth and runs to Joe Binham. Joe Binham's son is very excited. He puts the hamsters into a big box. On Sunday he gives Mick and Pam to his friend Charles as a birthday present.

Do you like this ending?
No? Okay, here is another one.

Ending number 3:

Dave runs deep into the wood. There he hears a cuckoo. The cuckoo is in a very big tree. Dave shouts: "Cuckoo, have you got a nut for me? I'm very hungry." The cuckoo says, "The squirrel has got a lot of nuts." Then the cuckoo shouts, "Fred, come out." Fred, the squirrel, comes out of his hole. Dave tells his story. Fred goes back into his hole and brings out a lot of nuts. "You can live in our tree," say the cuckoo and the squirrel. Dave is very happy. They tell a lot of stories and eat nuts.

6 ★

Here is a reading puzzle for you.
It is by 11-year-old Cynthia Brown from Cambridge.
Try to read the text, but do not write in the missing letters.
Then listen to the cassette and check.

Cynthia Brown

Mi__ an_ P_m ea_ al_ the nut_. Da__ i_ ver_ sa_. H_ go__ in__ th_ woo__ a__ mee__ Lilly, th_ fo_. "Wh_ d_ yo_ loo_ s_ sa_?" Lilly as__. "I ha__ go_ a bi_ proble_ wi__ m_ frien__ Mi__ a__ P__," Da__ sa__ a__ tel__ Li__ th_ st___ of th_ bo_ of nu__. Li___ list___ t_ Da__ a__ th__ sh_ i_ ve__ quie_. "Wai_ fo_ m_, Da__," sh_ sa__. "Mayb_ I ca_ hel_ yo_." Lil__ ru__ t_ th_ po__. Mi__ a__ Pa_ ar_ sit___ und__ a b__ tr__. "You'r_ no_ ver_ ni__ t_ Da__. Whe__ a__ al_ th_ nu___?" sh_ ask_. "Yo__ frie__ Da__ i_ ve__ s__," sh_ sa__. Mi__ an_ Pa_ lo__ a_ Lil__. "W_ ar_ ve__ sorr_," the_ sa_, "wha_ ca_ w_ d_?" "G_ an_ fi__ som_ nu__ an_ gi__ the_ t_ Da__," Lill_ sa__. Mi__ an_ P__ lo__ fo_ nu__. Lil__ hel__ th__. Th__ the_ al_ g_ ba__ in__ th_ woo__ whe__ Da__ i_. "We'__ sor__," Mi__ an_ Pa_ sa_ an_ gi__ Da__ th_ nu__. "O_, tha__ yo_," Da__ sa__. "No_ yo_ ca_ b_ frien__ aga__," Lil__ sa__ a__ smil__.

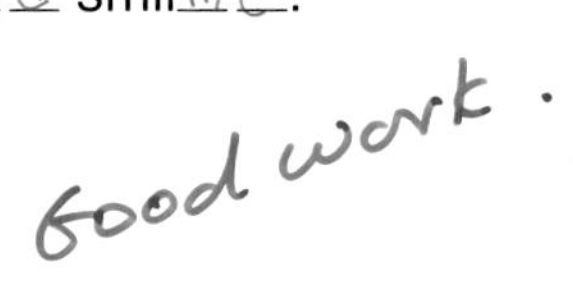

7 ★

Do you like Cynthia's ending?
No? Please write your own ending.

8

Now listen to the story "The box of nuts" on cassette.
Then work in groups. Act out the story with the ending you like best.

Grammar

Let's . . .

How to make suggestions:

Let's eat the nuts now.
Let's go swimming in the pond.
Let's go.
Let's ask the squirrel for some nuts.

UNIT 20

The great magician

1 Picture dictionary

2 A play

Read the following play.

Frank Osbert, the great magician

A play in five scenes

Roles:

Patrick Linda Brian Sally Blackie, the dog Frank Osbert, the magician

Scene one

The children are in the park, playing with the dog.

Linda: Come here, Blackie.
Blackie: Woof, woof.
Patrick: Blackie, come on, come on.
Brian: What's he doing?
Blackie: Woof, woof.
Sally: I don't know. Let's go and see.

The children run over to the dog.

Patrick: What's that? Look, he's drinking it.
Sally: Ughhh. It's blue! It looks horrible.
Linda: Stop it, Blackie. Come here.
Blackie: Woof, woof.
Brian: Oh, look! He's shrinking!
Linda: Oh, poor Blackie.
Sally: Oh, no.

The dog shrinks to the size of a mouse. The children take the dog and run home.

Scene two

The children are at home.

Linda: What can we do?
Brian: I don't know.
Sally: Let's ask mum.
Patrick: No, mum can't help. She's not a magician.
Linda: Yes, of course! We need a magician.
Brian: A magician? How do we find a magician?
Linda: Let's look in the telephone book.

They look in the telephone book.

Patrick: Ah, look here: Magician . . . Mr Frank Osbert.
Let's phone him.
Linda: What's his telephone number?
Patrick: Five – nine – seven – three – one – four.
Linda: Okay. Five . . . nine . . . seven . . . three . . . one . . . four.
Mr Osbert: Frank Osbert, magician, can I help you?
Linda: Erm . . . We have a problem with our dog.
Can we come and see you?
Blackie: Woof, woof.
Mr Osbert: Yes, of course. Can you come at three o'clock?
Linda: Fine, thank you very much.

Scene three

The children are at the magician's house.
He is looking at the dog.

Mr Osbert: Oh yes, he's very small.
Blackie: Woof, woof.
Patrick: Can you help us, Mr Osbert?
Mr Osbert: Oh yes, this is not a great problem for
Frank Osbert, the great magician.
Give me that green bottle on the shelf.
Brian: This bottle here?
Mr Osbert: Yes.
Brian: Here you are.
Mr Osbert: Thank you.
Listen. Blackie must drink this at midnight.

Linda: At midnight? Okay. Thank you very much, Mr Osbert. Goodbye.
Mr Osbert: Goodbye.
Blackie: Woof, woof.

Scene four

It's midnight.

Sally: Okay, Blackie, good boy. Drink this.
Blackie: Woof, woof.
Linda: Good boy, Blackie. Good boy.
Brian: Oh, look. What's happening?
Patrick: Ohhhhh! He's turning into a fish!
Brian: Ugh! It's horrible.
Linda: Poor Blackie.
Sally: Oh, no.
Brian: Quick! Get a plastic bowl and some water.
Patrick: Here you are.

Scene five

The children are at the magician's house again. He is looking at the fish.

Mr Osbert: Oh dear, oh dear, oh dear.
Patrick: Can you help us, Mr Osbert?
Mr Osbert: Oh yes, this is not a great problem for Frank Osbert, the great magician. Give me that pink bottle on the shelf.
Brian: This bottle here?
Mr Osbert: Yes.
Brian: Here you are.
Mr Osbert: Thank you. And give me that yellow bottle on the table.
Sally: This bottle here?
Mr Osbert: Yes.
Sally: Here you are.
Mr Osbert: Thank you. Now look. A little bit of this, and a little bit of that.

The magician opens the pink bottle and the yellow bottle and pours it all into the plastic bowl.

Mr Osbert: Abracadabra, wizzy wish, I want a dog and not a fish.
Sally: Oh, it's Blackie again.
Brian: But his ears are pink!
Patrick: And his nose is yellow.
Mr Osbert: Oh dear, oh dear, oh dear. Erm . . . I'm sorry.
Linda: He looks horrible. Pink ears and a yellow nose.
Brian: Oh, poor Blackie.
Sally: Oh, no.
Linda: Mr Osbert, we don't want a dog with pink ears and a yellow nose. He looks horrible!
Blackie: But I like it. I'm the only dog with pink ears and a yellow nose.
Children: Gosh! He can speak.

3

Make the sentences and write in the numbers.

1	The children are in the park	6	magician's house. ✓
2	Blackie drinks	4	and run home. ✓
3	Then he shrinks	2	something blue. ✓
4	The children take their dog	11	into Blackie again. ✓
5	In the telephone book	14	his pink ears and his yellow nose. ✓
6	They go to the	7	a green bottle. ✓
7	Mr Osbert gives the children	9	go back to Mr Osbert. ✓
8	At midnight Blackie	1	playing with their dog. ✓
9	Next morning the children	5	they find a magician's number. ✓
10	The magician opens a pink	13 12	he looks horrible.
11	The fish turns	8	turns into a fish. ✓
12	But Blackie	10	and a yellow bottle. ✓
13	The children think	3	to the size of a mouse. ✓
14	Blackie says that he likes	12 13	has got pink ears and a yellow nose.

4 A song

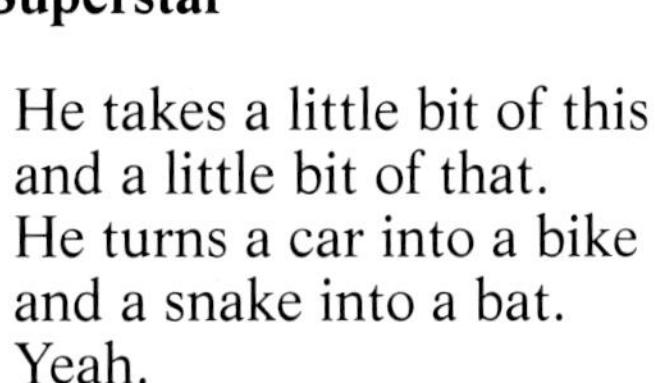

Frank Osbert Superstar

Chorus:

Have you got a problem?
Get into your car.
Come and see Frank Osbert.
He's a superstar.

He takes a little bit of this
and a little bit of that.
He turns a dog into a fish
and a mouse into a cat.
Yeah.

(Chorus)

He takes a little bit of this
and a little bit of that.
He turns a car into a bike
and a snake into a bat.
Yeah.

(Chorus)

He takes a little bit of this
and a little bit of that.
He turns a nose into an ear
and a parrot into a rat.
Yeah.

(Chorus)

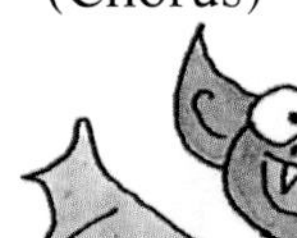

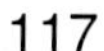

Listen to the play on the cassette.
Then work in groups and act out the play.
There are six roles.

Study and change

Read the texts below.
Write your own text and draw a picture of your friend, the magician.

Text 1

I have a friend. Her name is Priscilla Hocuspocus. She is a magician and she lives in an old tree. I like Priscilla very much. She sometimes turns me into a fish. That's great. I like swimming.

Text 2 ★

I know a magician. He lives in an old house behind the mountains. He is my best friend. His name is Silvester Wizz. Silvester Wizz is a great magician. In his house he has got a big old cupboard. There is a blue, a pink and a yellow bottle in it. When you drink from the blue bottle, you turn into a bird. When you drink from the pink bottle, you turn into an elephant. And when you drink from the yellow bottle, you turn into a crocodile. The yellow bottle is my favourite.

Grammar

this – that

How to refer to something near:

Do you want **this** bottle here?

How to refer to something farther away:

Give me **that** yellow bottle from the shelf.

Use the same words to refer to people:

Fred, **this** is Julia.

That's my English teacher over there.

UNIT 21

The elephant, the hippo and the mouse

1 Picture dictionary

2

Look at the picture and find out what the animals say.
Draw lines.

Willie, the hippo:

Fred, the mouse:

George, the elephant:

Fred, the mouse:

George, the elephant:

Fred, the mouse:

Good morning, Fred. Here's your apple.

No, thank you.

Thank you, Willie.

Anything else?

Good morning, Fred. Here's your cheese.

Thank you, George.

3 A story

Read the story.

The elephant, the hippo and the mouse

Far across the sea there is a small island. The island is the home of three animals: George, the elephant, Willie, the hippo, and Fred, the mouse. The island is very nice. George and Willie are always happy. They like living there. They play and dance in the sand.

But Fred is not happy. He must cook for George and Willie, make their beds and sing for them. Fred does not like this, but he must do what they say. The elephant and the hippo are so strong.

One night Fred makes a plan. He wants to play a trick on George and Willie. Early next morning he gets a long rope and puts it in the sand. He starts at the hippo's house. He pulls and pulls. Up the hill and down the hill. Soon the long rope goes from the hippo's house to the elephant's house. "Fred," the elephant shouts, "I'm hungry. I want eighty bananas and ten bottles of juice. I'm strong, so I must eat a lot." The mouse says, "You are not strong. I'm stronger than you." "Ha, ha," the elephant begins to laugh. "You are not stronger than me. You are a tiny mouse." "Yes, I'm stronger," the mouse says. "Let's pull the rope and see who is stronger."

The mouse ties the end of the rope round the elephant's leg and runs to the other end of the island. Willie, the hippo, is at home. The mouse says, "I want to have my breakfast. I want eighty bananas and my ten bottles of juice." "You . . . you . . . you . . . want eighty bananas?" the hippo asks the mouse. "Yes, I am very strong and so I must eat a lot," the mouse says. The hippo begins to laugh. "Ha, ha, you, the tiny mouse? You are not strong!" The mouse says, "I'm stronger than you!" "You?" the hippo says. He looks at the mouse and shakes his head. "Yes, I'm stronger than you," the mouse says. "Let's pull this rope and see who is stronger." The mouse ties the rope round the hippo's leg and runs to the top of the hill. "Pull!" the mouse shouts to George and Willie. The elephant and the hippo pull and pull. They pull and pull and can't understand it. What a strong mouse. After an hour they feel very tired. They lie down in the sand and fall asleep.

When the elephant wakes up, he thinks, "The mouse is stronger than me." And the hippo says to himself, "The mouse is stronger than me!" And from that time on Fred is very happy. George and Willie are very friendly. They always bring Fred's breakfast: a little piece of cheese and an apple. And Fred likes this.

4

True or false?

- The elephant, the hippo and the mouse live in the jungle.
- George is happy, but Willie and Fred are sad.
- Fred must cook and make the beds for George and Willie.
- Fred wants to play a trick on the hippo and the elephant.
- Willie and Fred put a long rope in the sand.
- The rope goes from Fred's house to George's house.
- The elephant wants eighty bananas and ten bottles of juice for breakfast.
- Fred ties the rope round the elephant's leg.
- The hippo wants eight bananas and six bottles of juice for breakfast.
- On the top of the hill the mouse shouts, "Pull!" to George and Willie.
- The elephant is stronger than the hippo.
- So the hippo brings breakfast for the mouse and the elephant.

5

Put the sentences in the correct order.
Number them 1 to 7.

- One day Fred plays a trick on the elephant and the hippo. He gets a long rope and puts it in the sand. The rope goes from Willie's house to George's house.
- When they wake up, they think, "The mouse is stronger." From that time on they always bring Fred his breakfast.
- There he tells Willie that he is stronger than the elephant. Willie shakes his head. Fred ties the rope round Willie's leg and runs to the top of the hill.
- George and Willie are happy and they play and dance in the sand. But Fred is unhappy because he must cook for George and Willie and make their beds.
- "Pull!" Fred shouts to George and Willie. George and Willie pull and pull, but after an hour they are very tired and fall asleep.
- Fred goes to George's house and says that he is stronger than the hippo. George laughs. Fred ties the rope round George's leg and runs to the other end of the island.
- George, the elephant, Willie, the hippo, and Fred, the mouse, live on a small island.

6

Now listen to the cassette.
Work in groups.
Act out the story.
There are four roles: the narrator, the elephant, the hippo and the mouse.

7 A story

Look at the pictures. Tell the story and find your own ending. Use the words in the box below. Then listen to the cassette.

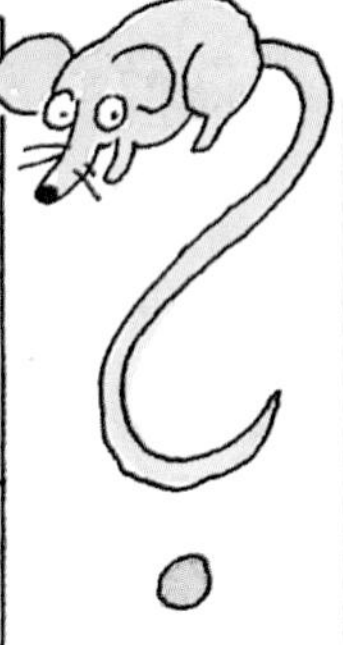

There is . . .
One day Fred wants to . . .
At night . . .
That night there is . . .
Fred shouts . . .
But George and Willie . . .
The next morning . . .

Grammar

must

How to express what someone must do:

I **must** eat something. I'm very hungry.
"You **must** marry the sun."
He **must** cook for George and Willie.
She **must** do her homework before she watches TV.

We **must** get up early in the morning.
You **must** go to bed now!
The children **must** go to school now. It's late.

UNIT 22

1 Grammar rhythm

Fill in the blanks.

I am	–	I was	take	– took
they are	–	they were	go	– went
have	–	had	see	– saw
listen	–	listened	jump	– jumped
play	–	played	say	– said
give	–	gave		

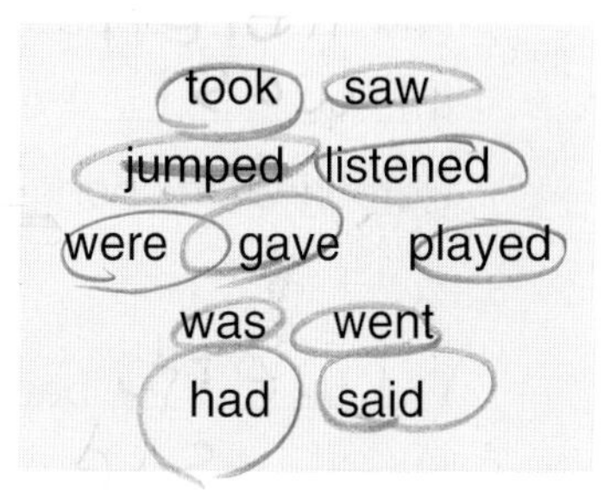

2 A song

Listen and fill in.

Peregrine, the penguin

Yesterday I had a dream.
I saw a little penguin.
His name was Peregrine.
It was Peregrine, Peregrine,
Peregrine, the penguin.

Peregrine, the penguin,
took me to a swimming pool.
The pool was full of orange juice,
and that was really cool.
It was Peregrine, Peregrine,
Peregrine, the penguin.

There were ten other penguins.
They all sad hey, hey, hey.
We have a super band.
Let's rock and roll today.
It was Peregrine, Peregrine,
Peregrine, the penguin.

Peregrine, the penguin,
took me by the hand.
We jumped into the swimming pool
and listened to the band.
It was Peregrine, Peregrine,
Peregrine, the penguin.

I went back home at eight.
My mum sad, "Time for school."
I sad, "Where are the penguins?"
Their band was really cool.

Now I'm on my way to school.
What's that behind the tree?
It's Peregrine, the penguin.
He wants to come with me.

It's my little penguin.
His name is Peregrine.
It's Peregrine, Peregrine,
Peregrine, the penguin.

Peregrine's Penguin Band

3

Read through the sentences about Martin's birthday party.
Match them with the pictures and fill in the correct numbers.

- [4] My sister gave me a new football.
- [3] We listened to the new cassettes.
- [7] At my party we had hamburgers, apple juice and ice cream.
- [8] I took my first photos with my new camera.
- [11] I had a big birthday cake with eleven candles on it. They were red, blue, green and yellow.
- [12] My friends gave me some books, some stickers and some cassettes.
- [9] My birthday was on the 15th of April.
- [10] This is the best photo. It is Susan.
- [6] We played with my new football.
- [2] I had nine presents.
- [1] Then we went out into the garden.
- [5] Dad gave me a camera.

4

★

Listen to the cassette. Martin is boasting about his party to a friend.
Mark the pictures ☒ that are different from what Martin says.

Picture 1	☐	Picture 4	☐	Picture 7	☐	Picture 10	☑
Picture 2	☐	Picture 5	☐	Picture 8	☐	Picture 11	☑
Picture 3	☐	Picture 6	☑	Picture 9	☑	Picture 12	☑

5

★

Say which pictures are different from what Martin said.
Say what really happened.

Picture [. . .] is different. | Martin had [. . .]. | His father gave him [. . .].

Pronunciation

Listen and repeat. Then practise in groups of three.
Speak as fast as you can.

A: Water! Water!
Where's some water?
B: Where is what?

A: Water! Water! I want water!
B: We all want water!
C: I want coke!

Study and change

Text 1

Yesterday I had a dream.
In my dream I had a big party.
There were twenty children
at my party. They gave me
lots of presents:
a computer game,
a camera, juggling balls and
five or six cassettes.
We listened to the new
cassettes.
Then we went out
into the garden and played.

Text 2 ★

Yesterday I had a dream. I saw
a little monkey. His name was Fips.
He took me to the jungle. It was great.
I saw lots of animals: crocodiles,
snakes, parrots and other monkeys.
All the animals were very nice to me.
When we said goodbye, Fips gave me
a wonderful present: a red and
yellow flower.
I was very happy about this present.

Grammar

Past simple

If you talk about the past, you usually use the past simple. You often use the past simple with expressions of time, e.g. yesterday, last week, etc.

Regular forms:

listen – listen**ed**
jump – jump**ed**
play – play**ed**

Irregular forms:

is – **was**		see – **saw**	
are – **were**		take – **took**	
have – **had**		give – **gave**	
say – **said**		go – **went**	

Yesterday I **had** a dream.
Peregrine, the penguin, **took** me to the swimming pool.
There **were** twenty children at the party.

UNIT 23

The pink racket

1 *Look at the pictures. These people are in the story "The pink racket". What do you think the story is about? What do you think happens in the story?*

2 A story

Read the following story.

The pink racket

Helen's family loved tennis. Her mother and father loved it, her younger brother loved it too, and her older brother was a very good player. At the weekend her family often played tennis. "Come along, Helen," they said, "it's great fun." So Helen watched her family play, but she was bored. She didn't like tennis. She liked reading detective stories or watching detective films on TV.
On Helen's birthday her father gave her a big box. In it there was a pink tennis racket. On Saturday Helen and her family went to play tennis. "This is Miss Richardson, your coach," her father said. Then her father, her mother and her brothers went away to play together. Helen hated playing with her coach. She really hated tennis.
When the family got home in the evening, Helen went to her room. She looked at her tennis racket. "What a stupid present! I'd like to smash it!" she said to herself. But then she put the racket back in the box with this note:

Thanks for the racket, dad, but I really don't like playing tennis.

Then she put it on her father's desk.
On Sunday her father found the box with the tennis racket in it. He put it away in a cupboard, but did not say a word to Helen. After that, at weekends, Helen's family no longer said, "Come along, it's great fun." And Helen sat in her favourite chair and read her detective stories or watched TV.

3

Make the correct sentences.

1	Helen's family often	◯	her family play tennis.
2	She watched her family	◯	read or watched TV.
3	She liked reading stories or	◯	the box on his desk.
4	Her father gave her a tennis	◯	play, but she was bored.
5	Helen did not like playing	◯	played tennis at weekends.
6	At home she put the	◯	racket for her birthday.
7	Her father found	◯	watching detective films on TV.
8	Helen no longer watched	◯	tennis with her coach.
9	She stayed at home and	◯	racket back in the box.

4

Talk about the story.

I [like / don't like] the story.

I think it [is OK / isn't OK] that they say, "Come along, Helen. It's great fun."

Dad's birthday present [is / isn't] a good idea.

Helen doesn't want to play tennis. I [can / can't] understand that.

Helen's family no longer says, "Come along, it's great fun." I think that [is / isn't] good.

I [like / don't like] the ending because [. . .].

5 ★

Read through the dialogue between Helen and two friends.
Fill in the gaps with the words in the box.
Then listen to the dialogue.

give	hate
know	doesn't
gave	now
back	him
angry	why
what	how

Penny and Robert: Hi, Helen.
Helen: Oh, hi.
Penny: __________ was your birthday?
Helen: It was alright, but my dad __________ me a stupid present.
Robert: Stupid? __________ was it?
Helen: A pink tennis racket.
Penny: __________ is that stupid? I'd like a tennis racket.
Robert: She __________ like tennis.
Helen: That's right. I __________ tennis.
Penny: Well, __________ the racket to me, then.
Helen: I can't. I gave it __________ to my dad.
Robert: You gave it back to __________? Was he __________?
Helen: I don't __________. I think so. He didn't say a word.
Penny: Not a word?
Helen: No. __________ I think he understands.
I really don't like tennis.

6 ★

Act out the dialogue.

Grammar

Some more past forms

Regular forms:		Irregular forms:	
love	– lov**ed**	do	– **did**
like	– lik**ed**	get	– **got**
hate	– hat**ed** [ɪd]	sit	– **sat**
watch	– watch**ed**	find	– **found**
look	– look**ed**	read [riːd]	– **read** [red]
		put	– **put**

UNIT 24

Greedy Oliver

1 Picture dictionary

2 A story

Look at the pictures. Then read through the sentences below. Match the sentences to the pictures. Write the correct number in each box.

Bad luck for Sally

- [6] She bought an ice-cream cornet.
- [2] Grandma gave her 50p.
- [5] She ran over to the ice-cream man.
- [9] A dog ate it.
- [1] Sally took her grandma's dog for a walk.
- [7] A big boy tried to grab her cornet.
- [3] Sally went for a walk in the park.
- [8] The ice cream fell onto the grass.
- [4] She saw an ice-cream man.

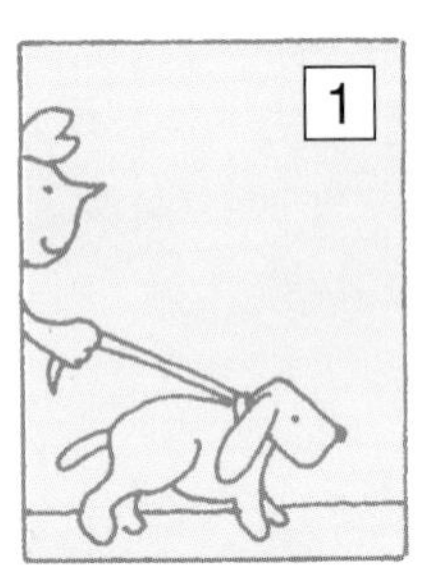

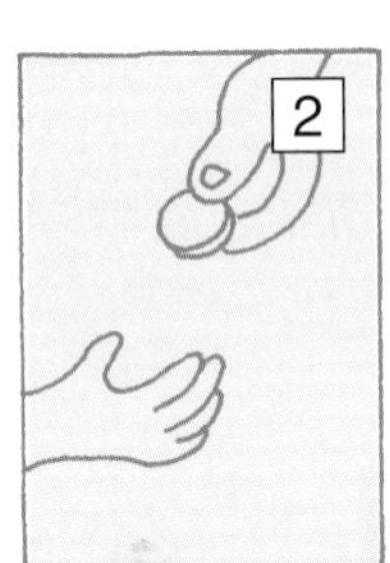

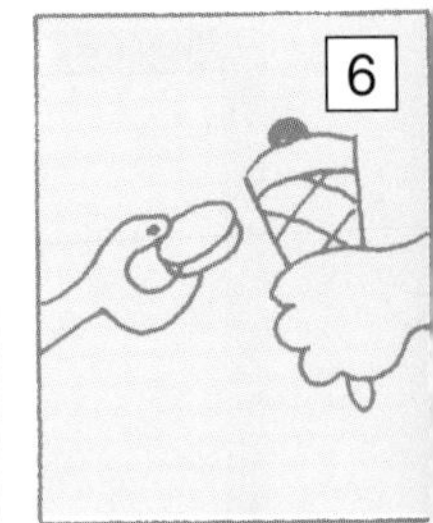

3 A story

Read the story.

Greedy Oliver

Oliver loved sweets: lollies, chocolate, ice cream and toffees. One day his grandmother gave him 50p. He quickly ran over to the sweet shop. There he bought a bar of chocolate. He ate the chocolate in the park. Then he thought, "Toffees. I'd like some toffees now."
So he went to Mrs Spencer's house and took her dog for a walk.
Mrs Spencer gave him 50p.
So Oliver bought a small bag of toffees. He ate the toffees in the park. Then he saw a girl eating an ice cream. And Oliver saw ice-cream cornets dancing before his eyes. He ran over to the sweet shop and hid behind the freezer.

When the shopkeeper turned her back, Oliver opened the freezer.
He tried to grab six ice-cream cornets and fell in. Bang went the lid of the freezer. The shopkeeper jumped and went over to the freezer. She waited for a minute. Then she helped Oliver out. He was freezing cold. The next time grandma gave Oliver 50p, he put it in his piggybank.

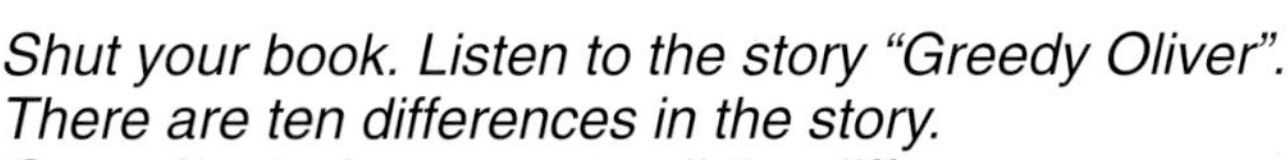

4

Shut your book. Listen to the story "Greedy Oliver".
There are ten differences in the story.
On a sheet of paper note all the differences you can spot.
Then listen again and check with the text in your book.

5

Look at the pictures and listen to the sentences.
The sentences are in jumbled order.
Write the number in each picture.

Text writing

★ *Look at the pictures and write what happened to Michael.*

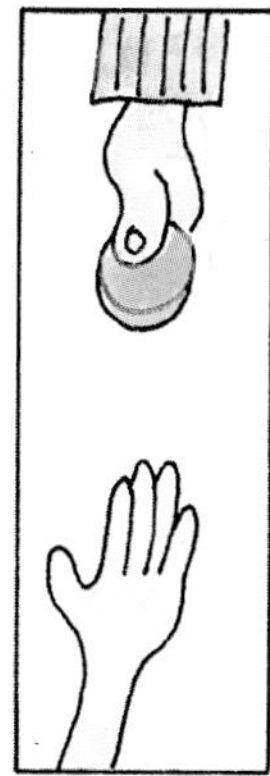

Begin your text like this: One day Michael took Mr Frazer's dog....

End your text like this: The girl gave him a kiss and he turned into....

Grammar

Some more past forms

Irregular forms:

eat – **ate**
buy – **bought**
fall – **fell**
hide – **hid**
run – **ran**
think – **thought**

Regular forms with particular spellings:

tr**y** – tr**ie**d (**y** becomes **ie**)
gra**b** – gra**bb**ed (doubling of consonant after short vowel)
sto**p** – sto**pp**ed

UNIT 25

What are you going to do?

1 Picture dictionary

2

Listen to the dialogues. Find out what the children are going to do.
✔ Tick the correct answers.

1

Ralph is going to

- [ ] watch TV in the afternoon.
- [ ] wash his dad's car in the afternoon.
- [x] play football in the afternoon

Jeff is going to

- [ ] do the shopping with his mother.
- [x] see his grandfather in hospital.
- [ ] play football with Ralph.

2

Claire is going to

- [x] stay in a hotel in London this weekend.
- [ ] visit friends in Scotland this weekend.
- [ ] have a party this weekend.

Jean is going to

- [ ] ask her dad about the weekend in London.
- [ ] ask her mum about the weekend in London.
- [x] ask her mum about the weekend in Scotland.

3

Grandma is going to	
☑	bake a cake with Philip.
☐	play cards with Philip.
☐	take Philip to the cinema.

Philip is going to	
☐	see his grandmother in hospital.
☐	play cards with his grandmother.
☑	help his grandmother bake a cake.

4

Sally is going to	
☐	play tennis on Saturday.
☑	have a party on Saturday.
☐	go to the Cup Final on Saturday.

Howard is going to	
☑	go to the Cup Final on Saturday.
☐	play football on Saturday.
☐	go to a party on Saturday.

3 *Make phone calls with a partner.*

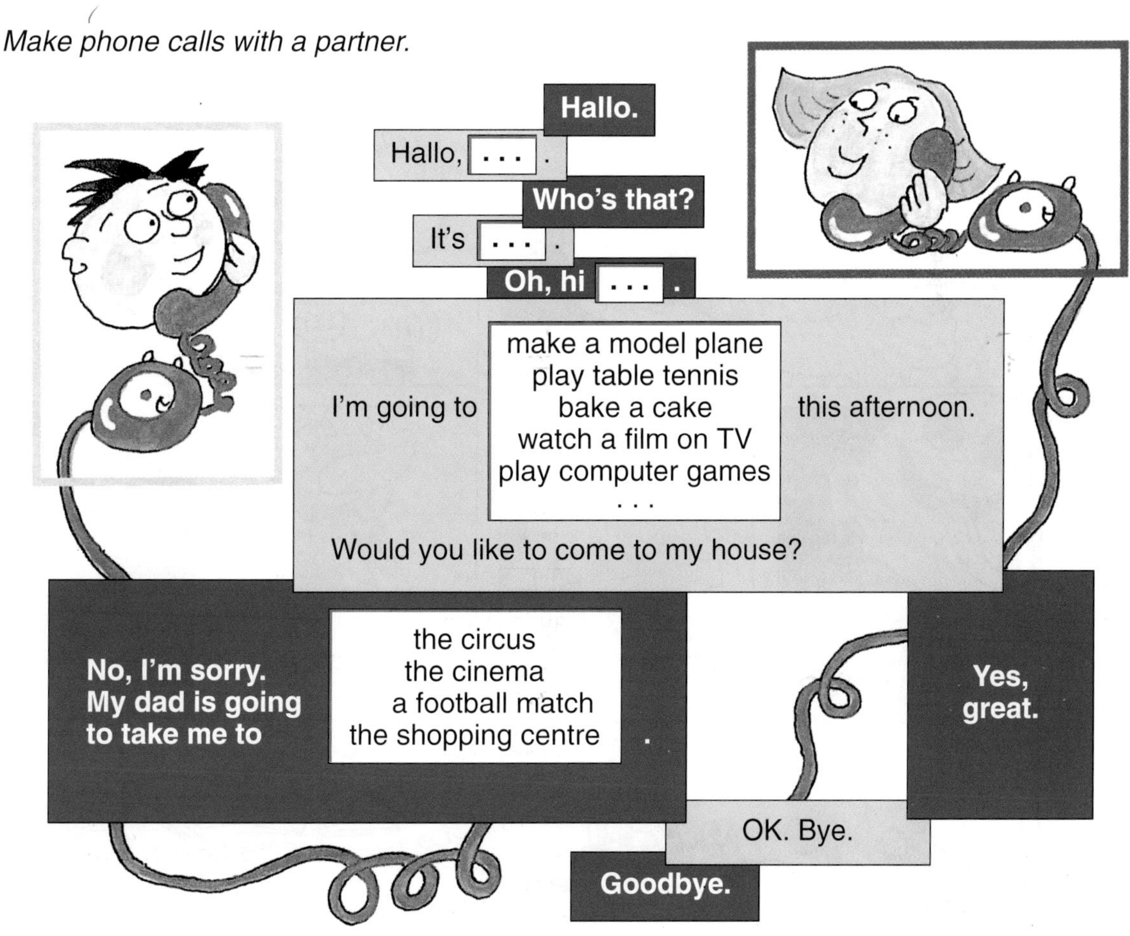

Hallo.
Hallo, ...
Who's that?
It's . . . .
Oh, hi . . . .
I'm going to
make a model plane
play table tennis
bake a cake
watch a film on TV
play computer games
. . .
this afternoon.
Would you like to come to my house?
No, I'm sorry. My dad is going to take me to
the circus
the cinema
a football match
the shopping centre
Yes, great.
OK. Bye.
Goodbye.

4 Grammar rhythm

Listen and fill in the missing words.

What ______ you ______ ______ ______? Just a sweet.
Who ______ he ______ ______ ______? You and me.
What ______ she ______ ______ ______? Come on, let's play.
Who ______ we ______ ______ ______? Don't ask me.
What ______ you ______ ______ ______? Sing with you.
What ______ they ______ ______ ______? That's it for today.

5

Listen to the second grammar rhythm. Put the pictures into the correct order by writing the numbers 1 to 10 in the boxes.

6 *Make the text with the help of the first letters and the pictures.*

★

W____ a____ y____ g____ t____ d____ w____ t____ ?

T____ ? T____ ?

I'____ g____ t____ l____ t____ o____.

W____ a____ y____ g____ t____ d____ w____ t____ ?

T____ ? T____ ?

I'____ g____ t____ f____ t____ .

W____ a____ y____ g____ t____ d____ w____ t____ ?

T____ ? T____ ?

I'____ g____ t____ c____ a ____.

W____ a____ y____ g____ t____ d____ w____ t____ ?

T____ ? T____ ?

I'____ g____ t____ g____ h____ s____ .

W____ a____ y____ g____ t____ d____ w____ t____ ?

T____ ? T____ ?

I'____ g____ t____ c____ . . . t____ .

Study and change

Text 1

At the weekend my dad
is going to take me to the cinema.
We are going to see "Jungle Jim".
Then we are going to have
double cheeseburgers
at the Burger Bar.

Text 2 ★

I like cooking, so this weekend
I am going to bake a cake.
I am going to give it to my grandma
because it is her birthday
on Sunday.
My mother is going to take her
to the theatre next week.
My grandma really loves the theatre.

Grammar

going to

How to express what you are planning or intend to do:

I'm going to make a model plane.
He's going to bake a cake for me.
She's going to take me to the cinema.
We're going to have a party next Saturday.
They're going to play tennis this afternoon.

How to ask what someone is planning or intends to do:

Where **are you going to** stay in London?
Are you going to play cards with us?

I"m going to sing a song for you.

Holidays

1 Picture dictionary

1. America
2. Mexico
3. Brazil
4. Argentina
5. Britain
6. Ireland
7. France
8. Spain
9. Germany
10. Italy
11. Sweden
12. Greece
13. Poland
14. Hungary
15. Turkey
16. Egypt
17. Nigeria

2

Look at the pictures of children and their names. Say where you think they are from.

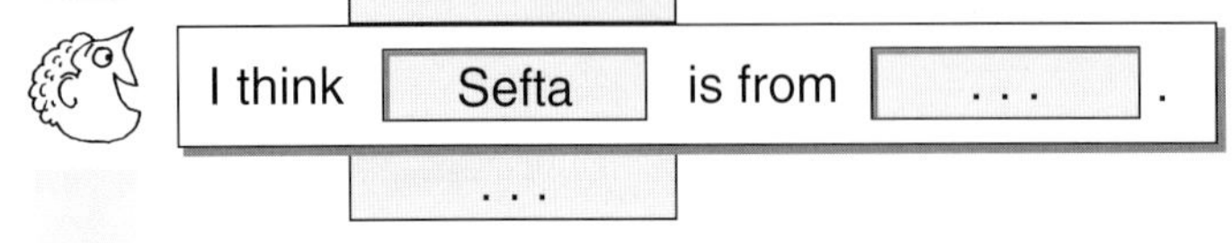

3

Look at the flags. Then say what you think.

★

Australian
Spanish
Italian
French
Turkish
Brazilian
Romanian
Polish
Argentinian
Japanese
Indian

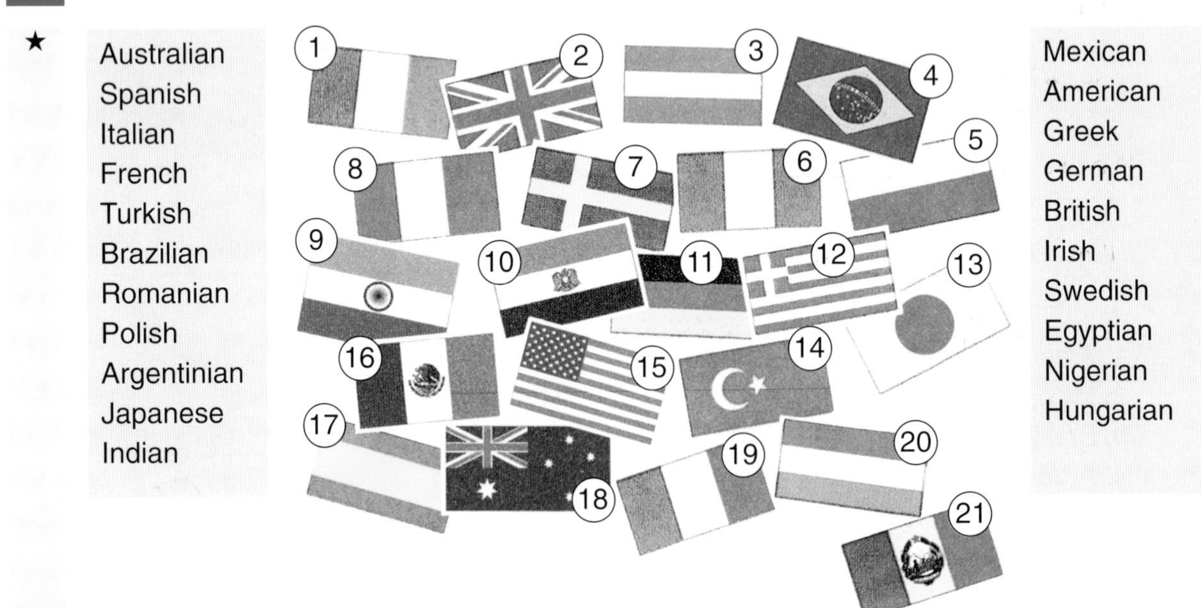

Mexican
American
Greek
German
British
Irish
Swedish
Egyptian
Nigerian
Hungarian

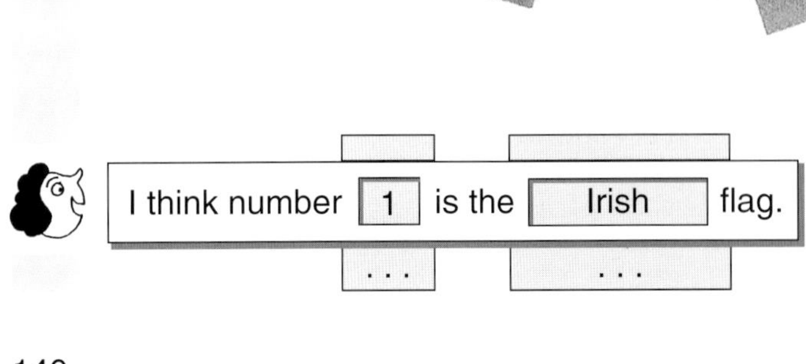

4

Listen to children in an international European summer camp. Fill in the boxes. Find out where the children come from and which are the flags of their countries.

	Country	Flag no.
Giovanni		
Brita		
Sefta		
Maria		

	Country	Flag no.
Kelly		
Pierre		
Patrick		
José		

Then say:

Kelly is from [Australia / . . .].

The [Australian / . . .] flag is number [. . .].

5 A song

Fill in the gaps with the words from the box. Then listen to the cassette and check.

A holiday in the USA

Yeah, a holiday in the USA,
a holiday in the USA.
Yeah, a holiday in the USA,
a holiday in the USA.

We're going to ____________ New York and New Orleans.
We're going to ____________ some T-shirts and some new blue jeans.
We're going to ____________ the Statue of Liberty.
What great fun for you and me.

Yeah, a holiday in the USA,
a holiday in the USA.
Yeah, a holiday in the USA,
a holiday in the USA.

We're going to ____________ some fun in Disneyland.
In Washington we're going to ____________ the President's hand.
We're going to ____________ the bears in San Diego zoo.
What great fun for me and you.

Yeah, a holiday in the USA,
a holiday in the USA.
Yeah, a holiday in the USA,
a holiday in the USA.

feed	see
shake	see
have	buy

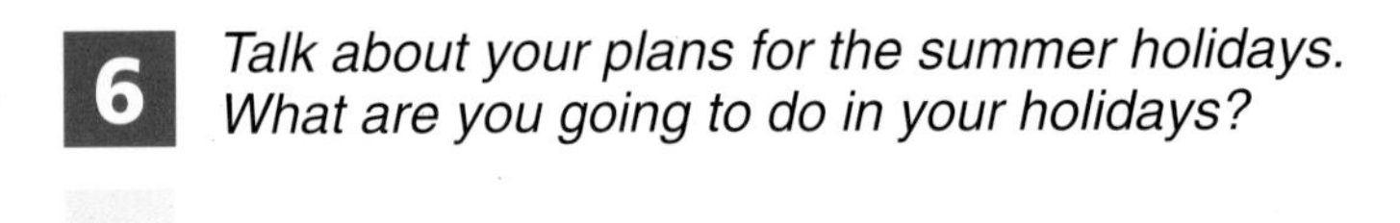

6 *Talk about your plans for the summer holidays.*
What are you going to do in your holidays?

spend . . . weeks in . . . with . . .
visit . . .
stay at home
go swimming a lot

I'm going to | go on a bike tour | .

go to . . .
sleep late and stay up late
play . . .
. . .

Study and change

Text 1

In my summer holidays
I am going to stay at home.
I am going to go swimming
a lot. I am going to sleep
late and stay up late.
I want to see all the good
films on TV. Mum says
I can watch them. I am also
going to play football
with my friends every day.

Text 2 ★

In my summer holidays I am going to spend
three weeks on a farm in the country.
There are lots of cows and horses.
And there are also two dogs.
I like animals a lot.
Then I am going to go to Mexico with
my parents and my little sister. I am going
to play and swim all day. I think Mexico is
great. The last five weeks I am going
to stay at home. I am going to read a lot.
My father says he is going to make
a tree hut for me. I think that's super.

Pronunciation table

- [iː] key, scene, sea, green, week
- [ɪ] village, give, big, fish finger
- [i] happy, lucky, really, thirty
- [e] bed, friend, ready, left, head
- [æ] plan, dad, match, fantastic
- [ɑː] father, basket, arm, party
- [ɒ] hot, sock, shop, watch, John
- [ɔː] door, floor, more, talk, warm
- [ʊ] book, football, good, put, would
- [uː] shoe, two, blue, cuckoo, June
- [ʌ] young, some, does, butter, brother
- [ɜː] girl, curtain, shirt, work, her
- [ə] colour, sticker, animal, about
- [eɪ] make, pay, name, radio, game
- [əʊ] know, old, programme, blow, oh
- [aɪ] eye, try, fine, crocodile, like
- [aʊ] now, mouse, cloud, blouse, how
- [ɔɪ] boy, toy
- [ɪə] here, idea, dear, fear
- [eə] hair, where, their, pair
- [ʊə] poor, tour
- [aɪə] tired, fire
- [aʊə] hour, our, flower
- [əʊə] lower
- [p] open, group, cup, peanuts
- [b] back, rubber, bottle, bedroom
- [t] tea, football, T-shirt, toast
- [d] day, don't, friendly, ending
- [k] school, clock, bike, key
- [g] ghost, bag, game, begin
- [tʃ] chocolate, watch, switch, chair
- [dʒ] jeans, German, generous, juice
- [f] half, shelf, feel, face, fun
- [v] very, village, have, live, five
- [θ] thing, third, think, mouth, bathroom
- [ð] the, there, with, mother, father
- [s] scene, glass, looks, pets, nice
- [z] was, zoo, trousers, apples, lazy
- [ʃ] show, shop, wash, shape, Finnish
- [ʒ] television
- [h] house, hippo, hide, hobby, hot
- [m] some, them, model, moment, money
- [n] nuts, know, present, Indian
- [ŋ] song, interesting, hang, darling
- [l] long, little, ball, plane, model
- [r] red, carry, sorry, wrist, run
- [j] yellow, yes, yoghurt, young
- [w] why, water, wait, want, sweets, one

Classroom communication

You have got problems – you say:

Sorry.
Can you help me, please?
Pardon?
Sorry, I don't understand.
Not so fast, please!
How do you spell that?
What's . . . in English, please?
Excuse me, can I ask something?
Can you help me with the exercise, please?
Sorry, I've forgotten (my exercise book).
Sorry, what's the homework?
Could you say it again, please?

Can you understand what your teacher says?

Who is absent?
Go and get me some chalk, please.
Would you clean the blackboard, please?
Would one of you hand these out, please?
Please collect the books, Christine.
Turn round, please.
Work in pairs/groups.
We are going to do some group work now.
What's the matter?
Quiet, please!
Speak up, please. I can't hear you.
Say it in English, please.
Can you say that in English, please?
Have you finished?
Put up your hand if you know the answer.
It's your turn now. Hurry up!
Come on, you can say it in English.
Come on, have a try!
Listen carefully.
Say it again, please.
Repeat this word, please.
All together now.
Get out your students' books/workbooks, please.
Open your books (at page . . .), please.
Close your books, please.
Listen to the cassette first.
Fine.
Well done!
Very good!
Excellent!
Good work!
Quite good!
You can do better than that.
That's not very good.
That's right.
Thank you very much.